# THE CHICAGO LAWYER ARTHUR JEROME EDDY AND HIS ECLECTIC ART COLLECTION

# THE CHICAGO LAWYER ARTHUR JEROME EDDY AND HIS ECLECTIC ART COLLECTION

Vivian Endicott Barnett

**American Philosophical Society Press**

**Philadelphia**

Transactions of the
American Philosophical Society
Held at Philadelphia
for Promoting Useful Knowledge
Volume 111, Part 2



ISBN: 978-1-60618-112-6
Ebook ISBN: 978-1-60618-117-1
U.S. ISSN: 0065-9746

Library of Congress Cataloging-in-Publication Data

Names: Barnett, Vivian Endicott, 1942- author. Title: The Chicago lawyer Arthur Jerome Eddy and his eclectic art collection / Vivian Endicott Barnett. Description: Philadelphia : American Philosophical Society Press, [2022] | Includes bibliographical references and index. | Summary: "This book describes the life of Chicago lawyer and art collector Arthur Jerome Eddy and details his extensive art collection"—Provided by publisher. Identifiers: LCCN 2022006027 (print) | LCCN 2022006028 (ebook) | ISBN 9781606181126 (paperback) | ISBN 9781606181171 (kindle edition) Subjects: LCSH: Eddy, Arthur Jerome, 1859-1920. | Art—Collectors and collecting—United States—Biography. | Lawyers—United States—Biography. | Eddy, Arthur Jerome, 1859-1920—Art collections. | Eddy, Lucy Crapo Orrell, 1863-1931—Art collections. | Chicago (Ill.)—Biography. Classification: LCC N5220.E33 B37 2022 (print) | LCC N5220.E33 (ebook) | DDC 709.2 [B]—dc23/eng/20220310 LC record available at https://lccn.loc.gov/2022006027 LC ebook record available at https://lccn.loc.gov/2022006028

Cover design by Eugenia B. González.

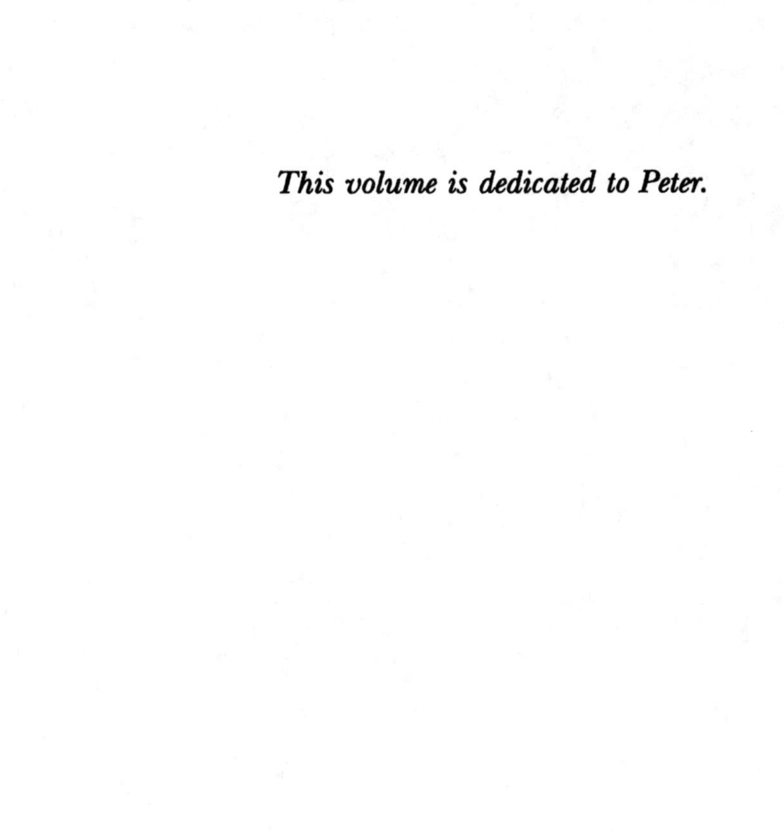

*This volume is dedicated to Peter.*

# Contents

# Acknowledgments

Research for the present volume took place over a ten-year period and took me many times to Chicago, also to Flint; Philadelphia; New Haven; Kansas City; Lawrence, Kansas; Los Angeles; Pasadena; Munich; and Paris. However, much of the work was done in New York under the auspices of the Center for the History of Collecting at the Frick Art Reference Library. I am most grateful to Inge Reist, Samantha Deutch, and Esmée Quodbach at the Center for sponsoring my work as a Leon Levy Fellow in 2010–11 and as a Senior Fellow in 2012. I would like to thank the staff of the Frick Library—especially Stephen J. Bury, Suz Massen, Ralph Baylor, and Louisa Wood Ruby—as well as the staffs of the New York Public Library, Watson Library at the Metropolitan Museum of Art, Museum of Modern Art Library, Whitney Museum of American Art Library, Beineke Rare Book and Manuscript Library at Yale University, the Library of the Art Institute of Chicago, the Newberry Library in Chicago, University of Chicago Special Collections, Chicago Public Library, Pasadena Public Library, and The Getty Research Institute. Recently I have benefited from the Wertheim Scholar Room at the New York Public Library.

At the Art Institute, Stephanie D'Alessandro, former Gary C. and Frances Comer Curator; Caitlin Haskell, the current Gary C. and Frances Comer Curator; Gloria Groom, David and Mary Winton Green Curator and present Chair of European Painting and Sculpture; and Bart H. Ryckbosch, Glasser and Rosenthal Family Archivist, have been exceptionally helpful. In Flint, Paul Gifford at the Genesee Historical Collections Library in the Frances Willson Thompson Library at the University of Michigan provided continued assistance. I am grateful to Frank Baron at the Max Kade Center at the University of Kansas at Lawrence for sharing his research on Albert Bloch and to Scott Heffley, former Senior Conservator of Paintings at the Nelson Atkins Museum of Art in Kansas City, especially for introducing me to Anna Bloch.

Sandra Boujot, Archivist at the Musée Rodin in Paris, was most helpful as was Véronique Borgeaud, Archivist in the Bibliothèque Kandinsky at the Centre Georges Pompidou. In Munich, Annegret Hoberg, Curator at the Städtische Galerie im Lenbachhaus, and Isabelle Jansen, Curator of the Gabriele Münter-und Johannes Eichner-Stiftung there assisted as always with my research. Among the many people (not cited in specific notes) who have been supportive, I would like to thank Paul Arculus, Carolyn Kinder Carr, Lynn Catterson, Mark Haxthausen, Josef Helfenstein, Angelica Jawlensky, Kirsten Jensen, Valerie Leeds, Sarah Kelly Oehler, Allison Perelman, Nancy Perloff, Eliot Rowlands, Judith Selkowitz, Gail Stavitsky, and Martin Tangora. Sean Weissbart provided invaluable help by searching legal databases. Peter Barnett designed and implemented a robust database into which I could enter all information about the works once in Mr. Eddy's collection.

I am not the first person to work on Arthur Jerome Eddy: Hans K. Roethel, Jean K. Benjamin, Courtney G. Donnell, Francis M. Naumann, and Paul Kruty have done research on the collector. I am grateful to Mr. Naumann for generously giving me his files and to Ms. Donnell for kindly sharing her research. Over the years, Stephanie D'Alessandro, Inge Reist, Samantha Deutch, and especially my family have been most supportive of this project.

I am grateful to Mary McDonald, Director of Publications at the American Philosophical Society, for her support since 2020 and to her successor, Alison Swety Beninato, and the team at APS in Philadelphia. Pamela Lankas of International Graphic Services conscientiously undertook the task of copyediting the manuscript and compiling the index. My thanks to Kerry Gaertner Gerbracht for obtaining the images and permissions for publication.

Vivian Endicott Barnett

# I

# Introduction

Arthur Jerome Eddy, the Chicago lawyer, author, and art collector, was a legend in his lifetime, which spanned the years from 1859 to 1920. His many accomplishments and enthusiasms make him appear to be over-the-top and all over the map. He was the first in many areas: the first to get a license plate for his automobile in Chicago in 1900, the first to buy radically modern paintings by Marcel Duchamp and Francis Picabia at the Armory Show in 1913, the first American collector to purchase works by Vasily Kandinsky and Paul Klee, and arguably the first person to write a book about modern art in this country. Not surprising, he gained the nickname *Mr. First.*[1]

A decade after Eddy's death, the former mayor of Chicago, Carter H. Harrison, Jr., recalled: "It was my good fortune to be a fairly intimate friend of Arthur Jerome Eddy, if not indeed a genius, a many-sided man who would have attained the highest rank in several endeavors other than the law where he took that standing, had he not, to use a colloquialism, 'spread himself over too much ground.'"[2]

As early as January 1901, upon receiving Eddy's book, *The Law of Combinations,* his friend, mentor, and fellow lawyer George R. Gold wrote: "While I know nothing of 'Eddy on Combinations', I suppose I did know him 'On' most everything else. The first thought upon tearing away the wrapping was: The author was a wonder and a wizard: What can he not do? There was Chess, Archery, Bicycling, Art, Poetry, Law, Song (?), Politics, Oratory, Money-Making, Courtesy—all the graces that are worth anything: he is like Saul among the children of Israel, 'head and shoulders above them all.'"[3]

Arthur Eddy was a corporation lawyer by profession and a partner in prominent Chicago law firms. He was instrumental in organizing American Steel Foundries, American Linseed Oil, National Carbon, and National Turbine, among other large corporations. He published his opinions on tariffs, bonds, trusts, and monopolies. Students of law and business are familiar with his books:

---

[1] Mrs. Jay Thompson in conversation with Courtney G. Donnell, May 15, 1976. I am grateful to Ms. Donnell for generously sharing her research. See also Madame X, "News of the Society World," *Chicago Daily Tribune,* January 9, 1910, B7.

[2] Carter H. Harrison, "Big Business Lawyer of Rebel Taste," *Chicago Evening Post,* December 29, 1931, 7.

[3] Letter dated January 23, 1901, from George R. Gold to Arthur J. Eddy, quoted in William V. Smith, ed., *An Account of Flint and Genesee County from Their Organization* (Dayton, OH: National Historical Association, 1924), 230.

*The Law of Combinations: Embracing Monopolies, Trusts, and Combinations of Labor and Capital; Conspiracy, and Contracts in Restraint of Trade* (1901) and *The New Competition: An Examination of the Conditions Underlying the Radical Change That Is Taking Place in the Commercial and Industrial World—The Change from a Competitive to a Coöperative Basis* (1912).

Nevertheless, a century later, Mr. Eddy is best known as a collector of modern art. Certainly he was quick to purchase paintings from the Armory Show (officially called the *International Exhibition of Modern Art*) soon after it opened in New York on February 17, 1913, and he bought more works later when the show traveled to Chicago. In all, he acquired eighteen paintings and seven prints from the show for a cost of almost $5,000. One reads that Eddy became an admirer of modern art after seeing the Armory Show and decided to go to Europe during that summer, where he met Kandinsky in Munich and bought the contents of his studio (or at least a large quantity of paintings) on the spot from the artist. None of these statements is true. Some myths—for example, that Eddy purchased Kandinsky's *Improvisation 27* and Duchamp's *Nude Descending a Staircase* at the Armory Show—have been disproved yet they keep reappearing. Other assumptions and "facts" are repeated because they remain difficult or impossible to verify. Research on Arthur Jerome Eddy has long been hindered by the loss of his papers: It requires painstaking detective work to separate fact from fiction. There are no records, receipts, diaries, or letters received.

The first works Eddy purchased when he went to the Armory Show in New York were Auguste Chabaud's *The Laborer* and Eugène Zak's *The Shepherd*. It is likely that he had seen both paintings—neither of which is shockingly modern—when they were exhibited earlier in Europe. Moreover, he may have already owned another painting by Chabaud. While Eddy acquired "extreme modern pictures" by European artists, such as Duchamp, Picabia, André Derain, Albert Gleizes, André de Segonzac, Amadeo de Souza Cardoso, Jacques Villon, and Maurice de Vlaminck, he also bought canvases by the Americans Leon Kroll and Edward Manigault. Some artists, such as Emilie Charmy or William Nicholson Taylor, were not well known at the time and have since been forgotten.

Inspired by the Armory Show, Eddy went to London and Munich with his wife and young son during the summer of 1913, where he purchased modern art and saw paintings that he would acquire the following year. Probably the greatest number and most significant acquisitions occurred in 1913–14: He purchased art from Russians living in Germany, such as Kandinsky, Alexei Jawlensky, and Robert Genin; from the Germans Paul Klee, Franz Marc, and Gabriele Münter; and from an American living in Munich, Albert Bloch.

Twenty years before the Armory Show took place, Arthur Jerome Eddy had begun to collect art. At the time of his death in 1920, he owned more than two hundred and fifty works—and not all were modern. In fact, his collecting was extremely eclectic or, as he expressed it, "catholic in taste." How he began to collect, when and from whom he bought art, which artists he favored, and why he acquired certain works and not others are some of the questions explored in order to solve the mysteries of Eddy's collection.

# II

# Family, Flint, and Education

Neither his family background nor his education suggests a familiarity with or tendency to collect art. Arthur Jerome Eddy was born in Flint, Michigan, on November 5, 1859, son of Jerome A. Eddy (1829–1905) and Ellen M. Curtis (1840–1933). His father, Jerome A. Eddy, was born in the town of Stafford in Genesee County, New York, and, as a young child, he moved with his parents to Flint in Genesee County, Michigan, in 1837. Jerome Eddy left school to work as a clerk in a general store: He became a merchant and, after the Civil War, went into the lumber business and then real estate. Arthur's paternal grandfather, Willard Eddy (1797–1861), was a carpenter by trade: He had traveled to Flint before settling there with his wife, Eliza Case Eddy (1805–92), and their children not many years after the town was founded by a fur trader in 1819. The northern region of Michigan was covered with dense forests and lumbering was the primary industry. Willard Eddy is said to have been one of the founders of the local bank. There is a portrait of him by an unknown artist in the Flint Institute of Arts, which was probably painted when he was about forty and lived in Flint. The face may have been copied from a daguerreotype and incorporated into the rather formal clothing.

According to the U.S. census from June 1860, Jerome Eddy was a thirty-one-year-old dry-goods merchant, who lived in Flint with his twenty-three-year-old wife, Ellen; seven-month-old son, Arthur; and an Irish servant. His real estate was assessed for $12,000 and his personal property at $8,000. Jerome's parents, Willard and Eliza Eddy, lived a few houses down the street. The Internal Revenue Service records for 1865 indicate that Jerome Eddy paid taxes of $2,111 on his income plus taxes on a carriage, a piano, and a watch. According to the 1870 census, Jerome was the proprietor of a sash factory: His real estate was valued at $33,000 and his personal property at $15,000.

No family memorabilia has come to light and no photographic images of Arthur Eddy as a young child are known. After attending local schools, he went to the Patterson School in Detroit:[1] presumably, Philo M. Patterson's School for Boys is intended. Because Detroit is sixty-five miles southeast of Flint, he may have boarded at the school. In September 1874 he enrolled as a member of the class of

[1] Letter dated January 23, 1901, from George R. Gold to Arthur J. Eddy, quoted in William V. Smith, ed., *An Account of Flint and Genesee County from Their Organization* (Dayton, OH: National Historical Association, 1924), 228.

1878 at St. Paul's School, a prestigious boarding school in Concord, New Hampshire. However, Arthur did not stay to graduate: He left St. Paul's in June 1876 when he was sixteen and a half years old.[2] The portrait by an unknown artist may have been painted at that time (Figure 2.1).[3] The oval picture shows a rosy-cheeked boy with dark-brown hair, blue-green eyes, a steady gaze, and firm chin. He wears a black jacket and tie, which contrast with the sitter's youthful appearance, his pink lips, and rosy complexion.

It is unclear where Arthur Eddy was and exactly what he did from June 1876 to September 1877. The Flint City Directory at that time listed him as a student living with his parents at the corner of Church and 5th Streets in the 3rd Ward.[4] His father owned a planing mill as well as a sash, door, and blind factory on Kearsley Street. In 1876–77, Jerome Eddy built the Eddy Block on Kearsley near South Saginaw Street opposite the Fenton Block. By June 1877 the upper part of the brick building had been rented: The law firm of Long & Gold took four rooms on the east side of the building, Gaskill & Thayer had "two elegant rooms on the west side, and the large rear room is to be occupied as a justice's office by Esquire Bickford."[5] A month later the newspaper reported: "We believe we are not exaggerating in the least to say that Long & Gold have the finest suite of rooms—four in number—for law offices, that can be found in the State. They have elegantly furnished them, and every appointment in their arrangement cannot be improved upon."[6]

The presence of so many lawyers is significant. It is not known when the Eddys became acquainted with George Ruggles Gold, who belonged to the same generation as Jerome. Gold (1830–1902) was from Connecticut and a graduate of Yale Law School with the class of 1856. Like Jerome Eddy, he was active in the Democrat Party and later served as mayor of Flint. In 1877 he was City Attorney in Flint and his law practice was in the Eddy Block. He became a good friend of young Arthur, who developed an interest in law.

On September 29, 1877, when he was seventeen, Arthur Eddy entered Harvard Law School in Cambridge, Massachusetts, as a

---

[2] Information kindly provided via email from David Levesque and Mary Jo Hansen of the Alumni Office of St. Paul's School, Concord NH, April 14–15, 2011.

[3] A note in the file for the painting (1940.1) at the Flint Institute of Arts by Mrs. George Wilson states that the portrait was probably executed c. 1874, when Eddy was sixteen or seventeen years old.

[4] The 1880 census recorded twenty-year-old Arthur as living with his parents at 622 Church Street in Flint.

[5] *The Sunday Democrat*, vol. XXIX, no. 49 (June 16, 1877): 1.

[6] *The Sunday Democrat*, vol. XXX, no. 1 (July 14, 1877): 1.

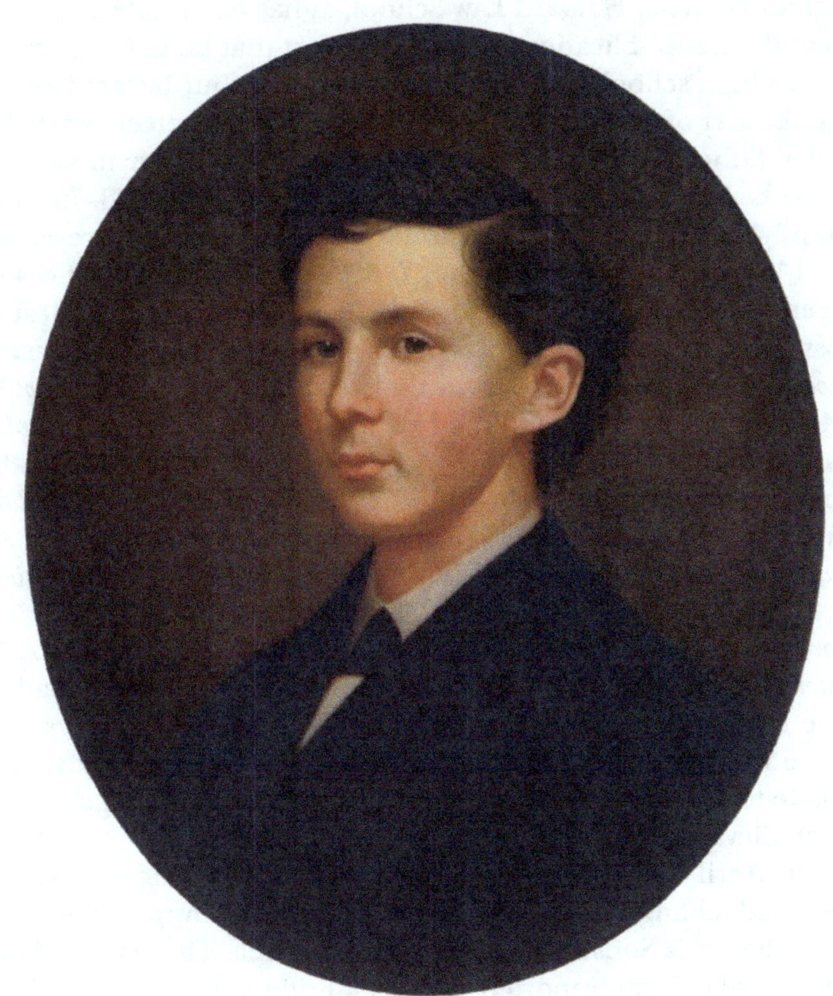

Figure 2.1 Unknown artist, Portrait of Arthur Jerome Eddy, c. 1876.
Flint Institute of Arts, Flint, Michigan: Gift of Jerome O. Eddy (1940.1).

special student. He studied there for only a year.[7] There is no indication that he went to college before attending law school; he did not study at Harvard College.[8] At that time a college degree

[7] *Quinquennial Catalogue of Officers and Students of the Law School of Harvard University*, 1888, 165.
[8] Confirmed via email from Harvard University Archives, January 25, 2011.

was not a prerequisite for admission to law school. Arthur Eddy did not graduate from Harvard Law School, as has been stated in *Who's Who* and other publications. Despite the fact that he did not graduate from high school, college, or law school, Arthur became editor and publisher of the *Genesee Democrat* when he was nineteen years old.

His father, Jerome Eddy, purchased the newspaper in December 1878 while serving one term as mayor of Flint (1878–79) and promptly appointed his son editor. The newspaper was previously owned by Horatio Nelson Mather (1827–1909) and had offices in the Fenton Block until late January 1879, when they were relocated across the street to the Eddy Block.[9] The Eddys published the *Genesee Democrat* and the *Sunday Democrat* and established the *Daily News* in 1884. In addition they published pamphlets: *The Farmer's Complete Encyclopedia: A Handbook of Universal Information* appeared in 1883. Arthur held the copyright to three publications in 1884: *A Plain Talk to Farmers about the Tariff*; *The Pith of the Tariff Question: An Inquiry into the True Relation between Wages and the Cost of Production*; and *"Come Let Us Reason Together." The Tariff: Facts and Figures for The Laborer, The Farmer, The Manufacturer.* In the pamphlet *"Come Let Us Reason Together,"* he addressed the larger issues of tariffs in relation to the cost of living for all Americans—not just free traders and protectionists—with charts and statistics. In 1884, Arthur Eddy was a delegate to the Democratic National Convention in Chicago, where Grover Cleveland was nominated for the presidency.[10]

On April 16, 1887, the *Genesee Democrat* announced that the paper had changed hands and that the new owners were W. H. Werkheiser & Sons from Easton, Pennsylvania. Three weeks later the personal column reported that, "A.J. Eddy is fitting up an office in the Eddy block on Kearsley Street in a handsome manner to be used by him in his law business."[11] Advertisements for the Baldwin & Eddy Law Office appeared in the *Genesee Democrat* from May 1887 through July 1888. Augustus Carpenter Baldwin (1817–1903) was considerably older than Arthur and lived in Pontiac (forty-five miles southeast of Flint). Baldwin, who had been admitted to the Michigan bar in 1842, was a member of the Michigan State House of Representatives (1844–46), a delegate to the Democratic National Convention

[9] Mather, who was originally from New York, owned several Michigan newspapers. He founded the *Michigan Sun* in 1879 in Detroit.

[10] Smith, ed., *An Account of Flint and Genesee County*, 229.

[11] *Genesee Democrat*, vol. XXXIX, no. 47 (May 7, 1887): 1.

in 1860, served as a Democratic representative in the Thirty-eighth Congress (1863–65), and was mayor of Pontiac in 1874.[12]

One reads that Arthur Eddy continued to study law with a local sage[13] and that he was admitted to the bar of Genesee County by Judge Newton.[14] But it remains unknown whether he studied with Judge William Newton or George Gold. William Newton (1822–1903) was a circuit judge in Flint (7th circuit) from 1882 to 1893 and active in the Democratic Party.[15] Young men are known to have read law with him, so Arthur Eddy may have studied with Newton. George Gold had offices in the Eddy Block and knew both Arthur and Jerome Eddy; moreover, his widow, Mary Gold, and daughter, Lillian, were named as beneficiaries in Arthur's will.

Augustus Baldwin lived in Pontiac, Michigan, but practiced law with Eddy in Flint in 1887–88. The Flint City Directory of 1888 listed the offices of Baldwin & Eddy at 1026 Church Street. It is probable that in the autumn of 1888, Arthur Eddy moved to Chicago, where he pursued his legal career. In early December 1888, he successfully argued a case before the Michigan State Supreme Court in which he represented his father in *Jerome Eddy v. Arthur McCall*. Mr. McCall had won the case earlier, but Mr. Eddy took an appeal to the Supreme Court, which ordered that the case be retried. After a two-day trial, the jury delivered a verdict in favor of Jerome Eddy.[16]

---

[12] The Political Graveyard, accessed February 23, 2019, http://politicalgraveyard.com/bio/baldwin.html and http://bioguide.congress.gov.

[13] Paul Kruty, "Arthur Jerome Eddy and His Collection: Prelude and Postscript to the Armory Show," *Arts Magazine* 61 (February 1987): 40.

[14] Edwin O. Wood, *History of Genesee County Michigan: Her People, Industries and Institutions* (Indianapolis, IN: Federal Publishing Company, 1916), 620.

[15] The Political Graveyard, accessed February 23, 2019, http://politicalgraveyard.com/newton.html.

[16] *Genesee Democrat*, vol. XLI, no. 18 (December 8, 1888): 4.

# III

## Move to Chicago, 1888; Law Practice; Activities; and Marriage

For the year 1888, Eddy's name appears in both the Flint City Directory and the Chicago City Directory. In Chicago, Arthur J. Eddy is listed as residing at 3834 Ellis Street and having an office in the Ashland Block, which housed many lawyers' offices.[1] By the following year, he lived at 4823 Lake Avenue and the firm of Walker & Eddy was located at 668 Rookery, a new tall building on S. LaSalle Street.[2] Eddy's partner, Edwin Walker (1832–1910), was born in Genesee County, New York (as was Arthur Eddy's father); he worked for several railroads in Indiana and Illinois before moving to Chicago in 1865. He was chosen to represent the Chicago Bar Association at the National Bar Convention in Washington, DC, on May 22, 1888. He and his wife, Mary, lived at 2612 Michigan Avenue. In 1889, Walker was appointed to the Executive Committee of the World's Columbian Exposition, became a member of the by-laws committee the following year, and served as Chairman of the Committee on Legislation. It is unclear when and how Edwin Walker and Arthur Eddy met, but the older, well-established lawyer opened many doors for Eddy.

The first mention of Arthur Eddy in Chicago newspapers occurred in October 1889, when he was appointed chairman of a debate at the seventh banquet of the Sunset Club. Organized in March 1889, the stated purpose of the Sunset Club was "to foster rational good fellowship and tolerant discussion among business and professional men of all classes."[3] The members met for dinner every other Thursday, followed by a discussion. On October 24, 1889, two hundred business and professional men attended and considered "The Sunday Question." The club's secretary. W. W. Caitlin, announced that Arthur J. Eddy was chairman of the debate and would present the opening remarks. According to the article in the *Chicago Daily Tribune*, Mr. Eddy took a broad view of the topic and stated: "If it is a day of rest, you know as well as I do that no two men agree as to what constitutes rest. How pernicious it is for us to dictate to others that they shall spend Sunday as we may think best. We tell some one that he must do on Sunday what is really work to him instead of rest. … I believe in giving the widest possible liberty to the observance of Sunday."[4]

---

[1] *The Lakeside Annual Directory of the City of Chicago* (Chicago: The Chicago Directory, 1888), 524.

[2] *The Lakeside Annual Directory of the City of Chicago* (Chicago: The Chicago Directory, 1889), 546, listed his home address as 4823 Lake Avenue, the same address was listed for 1890. As of 1892, Walker & Eddy was located at 616 Rookery and Eddy lived at 1718 Alexander Avenue.

[3] *The Sunset Club Yearbook* (Chicago: The Sunset Club, 1891), n. p.

[4] "For Sunday Observance," *Chicago Daily Tribune*, October 25, 1889, 5.

A few months later, in April 1890, he spoke at a meeting of the Sunset Club on "Drones and Parasites."[5] The next year he gave an address at an economic conference in Recital Hall titled "What Is Labor's Share?"[6] Eddy's skill and ability to debate probably go back to his studies at St. Paul's School, although there is no record of what courses he took during his two years there. Likewise, his year at Harvard Law School prepared him not only to argue cases in court, but also to persuasively debate a wide range of subjects.

The "Court Record" in the *Chicago Daily Tribune* lists a petition for condemnation filed in County Court by Walker & Eddy in the case of *Chicago & Pacific Railway Co. v. William B. Isham et al.*[7] From 1890 through 1892, most cases were filed in Circuit Court: *Cyrus D. Roy v. U.S. Rolling Stock Co.*; *W. P. Rend & Co. v. D. Kelley & Co.*; *E. C. Walker et al. v. M.B. Nerely and Nerely Commission Co.*; and *Edwin C. Walker et al. v. N. H., Charles C. and Cyrus T. Warren.*[8] In September 1892, Eddy was involved in an altercation with Theodore G. Case, attorney for Goldie & Son, in Judge Hutchinson's courtroom.[9] A few days later the newspaper reported that the difference between the two lawyers was "only a lively and animated legal one, the true character of which was well understood by them, and that Judge Hutchinson found no occasion to interfere in the matter."[10] Although records do not exist, it appears that Arthur Eddy was admitted to the Illinois Bar Association in 1890.[11] He may have been admitted to the Chicago Bar Association two years earlier. The year 1890 was a significant one for both his professional and personal lives.

Arthur Jerome Eddy and Lucy Crapo Orrell were married on June 3, 1890, in Flint by the rector of the Episcopal Church, Reverend A. W. Seabreze, assisted by Reverend Farnum. Lucy Crapo Orrell was the granddaughter of Henry H. Crapo (1804–69), who had been mayor of Flint (1860–61) and governor of Michigan (1865–69). Lucy was born in Flint on September 16, 1863, the daughter

[5] *Chicago Daily Tribune*, April 11, 1890, 3.

[6] *Chicago Daily Tribune*, March 30, 1891, 3.

[7] *Chicago Daily Tribune*, December 4, 1889, 10.

[8] *Chicago Daily Tribune*, November 23, 1890, 10; January 8, 1891, 9; March 10, 1891, 9; August 29, 1891, 14, respectively.

[9] "His Court-Room Not a Prize Ring," *Chicago Daily Tribune*, September 24, 1892, 3.

[10] *Chicago Daily Tribune*, September 27, 1892, 6.

[11] *Book of Chicagoans: A Biographical Dictionary of the Leading Men in the City of Chicago* (Chicago: A. N. Marquis, 1911), 208. The 1905 edition erroneously stated (p. 182) that Eddy was admitted to the Illinois Bar in 1880, but this was corrected in the 1911 and 1917 editions.

of Reverend John Orrell and his wife, Mary Ann Crapo Orrell. She grew up in Flint with her parents; her older sisters, Florence and Esther; and younger brother, William. Lucy, who was known as *Lulu*, spent the years from 1879 to 1882 at Lassell Seminary in Auburndale, Massachusetts. Records indicate that she was on the honor roll during her second year and that she studied instrumental music her freshman year (her third year there). She does not seem to have graduated yet Lulu later attended Madame Da Silva's French School on West 38th Street in New York, followed by six months' study abroad.[12] Remarkably little biographical information and no photographs of Lulu have been found. Both Robert Vonnoh and Nanette Calder painted her portrait, but neither picture has been located. The Eddys lived at 1718 Alexander Avenue in Chicago. Their only child, Jerome Orrell Eddy, was born on May 12, 1891.

Arthur Eddy played an essential role in organizing the Contributors' Club in late 1892 and he was the copyright holder and editor of the *Contributors' Magazine* in 1893–94. In the postscript to the first issue, he stated: "The plan of the Contributors' Club is to contribute, read and print, for members only, our own magazine. From contributions in hand will be selected such as will make each number as symetrical [*sic*], as harmoniously heterogeneous, so to speak, as possible, and in point of length, enough to occupy about one hour-and-a-half in the reading. On the evening of the meeting, each writer will read his own contribution, or select some member of the club to read it, as may be preferred. After the reading printed and bound copies of the magazine will be distributed. Such, in short, is the scheme of the club. So far as we know, it is novel. ... The Magna Carta of the Contributors' Club contains but one guarantee of liberty—to write when, where and what we please."[13] The first meeting took place on February 24, 1893, at the home of Mr. and Mrs. Charles Henrotin.

Earlier that year, on February 14, Eddy had written to the poet Harriet Monroe asking her on behalf of the Contributors' Club to invite the writer Henry Blake Fuller to join as an honorary professional member. Fuller accepted and sent an essay, "Holy Week in

[12] Information from Mary Orrell Willett's scrapbook preserved at the Genesee Historical Collections Center, Frances Willson Thompson Library of the University of Michigan at Flint and from the Winslow Archives at Lasell College in Newton, Massachusetts, transmitted by the Whaley House Museum of Flint, Michigan.

[13] *Contributors' Magazine* I, no. 1 (February 22, 1893): 35.

Seville," for the second issue. The founding members of the club included the poets Harold Heaton, Harriet and Lucy Monroe; the writers Hobart Chatfield-Taylor and Franklin H. Head; the publisher A. C. McClurg; the lawyers John W. Ela, Arthur L. Ryerson, and Alexander F. Stevenson. Arthur J. Eddy and Walter C. Larned were both writers and lawyers. It was the intention of the club to bring together businessmen and intellectuals. Among the businessmen were Augustus N. Eddy (not a relative), John J. Glessner, and James B. Waller. Moreover, the membership lists included many couples. Often the men were active in business and their wives contributed to the magazine: for example, Charles Henrotin was a stock broker and his wife, Ellen, was active in women's organizations—as was Mary Wilmarth. Prominent members of society, such as the Potter Palmers, Augustus N. Eddys, Arthur J. Catons, and Mrs. William Armour, were also members.

Each of the four issues of the *Contributors' Magazine* contained a postscript written by its editor, Arthur Eddy. As he explained in the first issue: "Our venture is founded upon the conviction that it is still possible for people to amuse themselves without the assistance of professional amusers. People are read, sung and played to, until they are played out. It is the fashion now-a-days, to provide entertainment for one's guests through which they are expected to sit, more or less silent, until an intermission gives relief or the thing is over; it is the most purpose of the members of the Contributors' Club to entertain themselves, each contributing after his own fashion, at his own pleasure, toward that end, and if we fail, we bore none but ourselves."[14]

Eddy's experience as an editor and publisher in Flint from 1878 to 1885 undoubtedly prepared him for his role in the Contributors' Club. His ability to write quickly and easily would continue throughout his lifetime. Not only did he write postscripts for the magazine but he also contributed two poems to the first issue and reviewed the World's Columbian Exposition for the third.

[14] *Contributors' Magazine* I, no. 1 (February 22, 1893): 35.

# IV

## World's Columbian Exposition, Early Collecting, and Posing for Whistler, 1894

Arthur Eddy's affiliation with both the Contributors' Club and with his law partner, Edwin Walker, undoubtedly heightened his interest in the Columbian Exposition. Through the club, he was in touch with Bertha Honoré Palmer, the President of the Board of Lady Managers of the Exposition and the undisputed queen of Chicago society. She and her husband, Potter, collected Impressionist paintings. It was at their home on Lake Shore Drive that Eddy read his review of the Exposition when the club members met on January 12, 1894.

Harriet Monroe was commissioned to write the "Columbian Ode" to be recited at the dedication of the exposition (known also as the *World's Fair*) on October 21, 1892. Six months later the huge exposition formally opened on May 1, 1893, and brought visitors from around the world to marvel at the immense grounds, imposing buildings, and countless exhibits until it closed at the end of October. The enormous success of the World's Fair transformed the city and inspired many collectors. Arthur Eddy became interested in art around the time of the Exposition. Harriet Monroe remembered that "the Columbian Exposition converted [Eddy]. Soon to our surprise, we would find him in its art galleries; and before they closed the collector's mania had caught him and he was showing exceptionally progressive taste in his numerous purchases."[1] His involvement with the Contributors' Club coincided with final preparations for the World's Columbian Exposition. Through the club he had contact with Bertha Palmer as well as her committee members, Ellen Henrotin and Mary Wilmarth. Moreover, his law partner, Edwin Walker, was not only on the Board of Directors but was also appointed Solicitor-General or Counsel to the Exposition. Thus, Eddy would have been well informed and well connected.

Eddy was particularly impressed by the prominently featured works of the American artist James McNeill Whistler and the French sculptor Auguste Rodin. Rather than simply purchase their art, he decided to commission Whistler to paint his portrait (Figure 4.1), and to have Rodin execute a portrait bust (Figure 4.2). In addition, Eddy acquired three pictures that were exhibited at the World's Columbian Exposition: *Marine* by Alexander Harrison, *Along the Mianus River* by Leonard Ochtman (Figure 4.3), and *Hagar and Ishmael* by Henry Oliver Walker (Figure 4.4). On January 19, 1894,

[1] Harriet Monroe, *A Poet's Life: Seventy Years in a Changing World* (New York: Macmillan, 1938), 116.

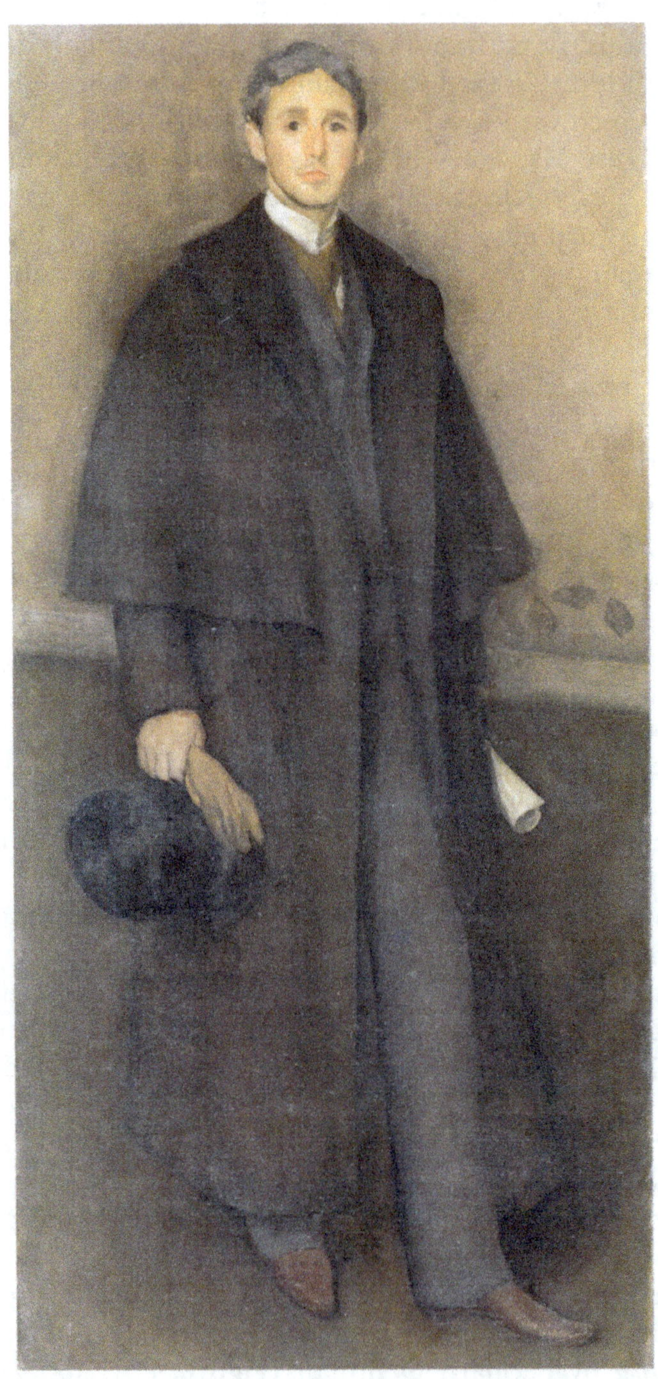

Figure 4.1 James McNeill Whistler, *Arrangement in Flesh Color and Brown: Portrait of Arthur J. Eddy*, 1894.

The Art Institute of Chicago: Arthur Jerome Eddy Memorial Collection (1931.501).

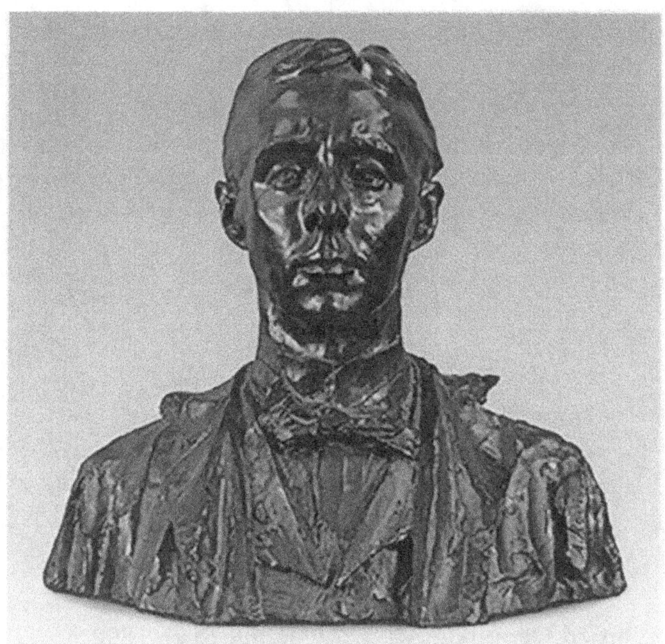

Figure 4.2 Auguste Rodin, *Bust of Arthur Jerome Eddy,* 1898.
The Art Institute of Chicago: Arthur Jerome Eddy Memorial Collection (1931.502).

he wrote to Mrs. Palmer indicating that he was about to buy an Ochtman painting and asked whether he might see the one she owned as the artist considered it to be one of his best.[2] Then in December 1894 or early 1895, he purchased Winslow Homer's *Coast of Maine* of 1893 (Figure 4.5), from the O'Brien Gallery in Chicago. Homer had exhibited fifteen paintings and was awarded a gold medal at the Exposition. The fact that Eddy purchased paintings by American artists at the time of the Exposition is often ignored. Moreover, he never sold these pictures since they were all listed in the estate inventory prepared after his death in 1920. In the 1890s Arthur Eddy's taste was eclectic, as the contrast between Homer's *Coast of Maine* and Whistler's *Arrangement in Flesh Color and Brown* makes overwhelmingly clear.

Whistler was also an American (born in Lowell, Massachusetts, in 1834), although he lived primarily in England and knew French

[2] Bertha Palmer Correspondence Collection, Series I, Folder 1.5, Ryerson and Burnham Library, Art Institute of Chicago.

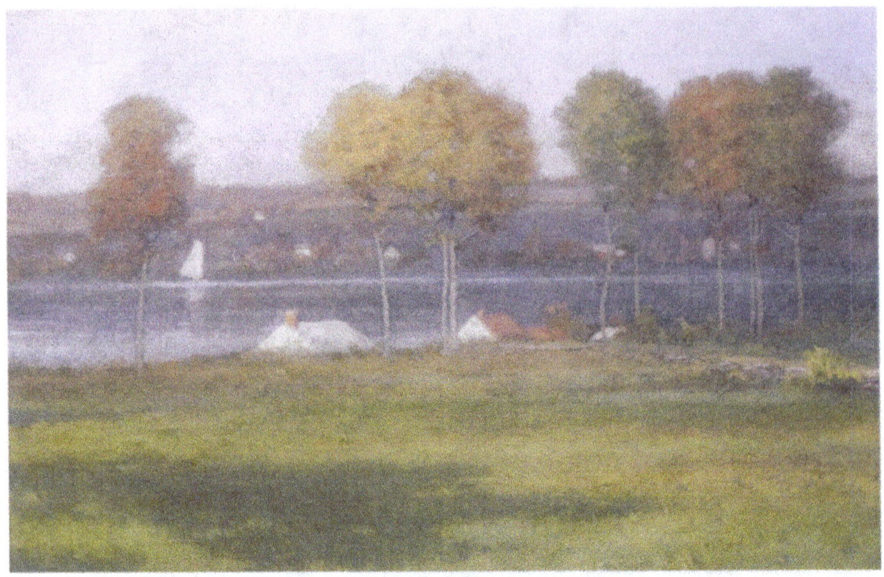

Figure 4.3 Leonard Ochtman, *Along the Mianus River*, 1892.

Flint Institute of Arts, Flint, Michigan: Gift of Mr. and Mrs. Jerome O. Eddy (1940.5).

artists before moving to Paris for several years. In September 1894, Eddy traveled to Paris, where he posed for Whistler every day for almost six weeks and began a lengthy and cordial correspondence with the artist. Eddy's portrait, *Arrangement in Flesh Color and Brown* (see Figure 4.1), was completed in October and installed in his Chicago home by December 1894. In a letter dated October 27 from the Grand Hotel in Paris, Eddy wrote to the artist: "Time is too short for me to adequately express all I feel toward you and Mrs. Whistler, but the few hasty words of parting to-night were entirely insufficient. … I realized to-day as I have not before the strain and misadventure under which you have been working all along—and more than ever I appreciate your very great patience. Ah well I can sum it all up by saying that as man and artist you have more than met my expectations. The portrait we own will be more than a portrait—or a picture—a memento of weeks delightfully spent in spite of personal discomfort and mental strain."[3] In another

[3] "The Correspondence of James McNeill Whistler," Letter E5, accessed March 16, 2019, http://whistler.arts.gla.ac.uk/correspondence.

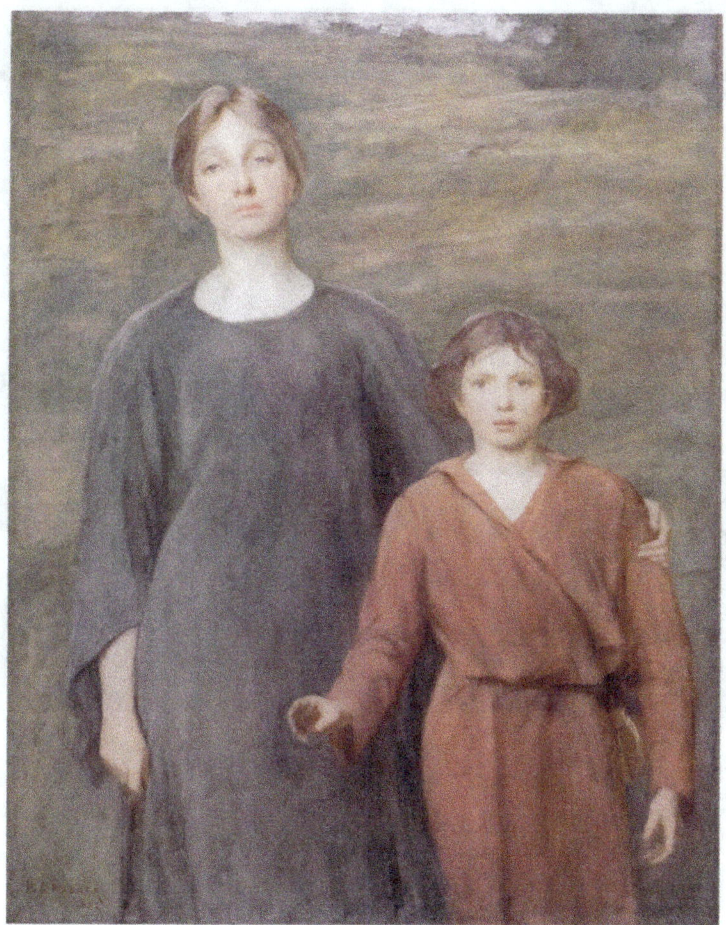

Figure 4.4 Henry Oliver Walker, *Hagar and Ishmael,* 1892.

Flint Institute of Arts, Flint, Michigan: Gift of Mrs. Arthur Jerome Eddy (1931.1).

letter to the artist he related: "Only last night I told Mrs. Eddy that you were the only man I ever met and associated with daily whom I found companionable and ever more enjoyable each succeeding day. Barring the pain and torture we had—perhaps I should say, I had—the best times together."[4]

After his return to Chicago, Eddy met in November with officials at the Art Institute, including the president, Charles Hutchinson,

[4] "The Correspondence of James McNeill Whistler," Letter E4 (incorrectly dated), accessed March 16, 2019, http://whistler.arts.gla.ac.uk/correspondence.

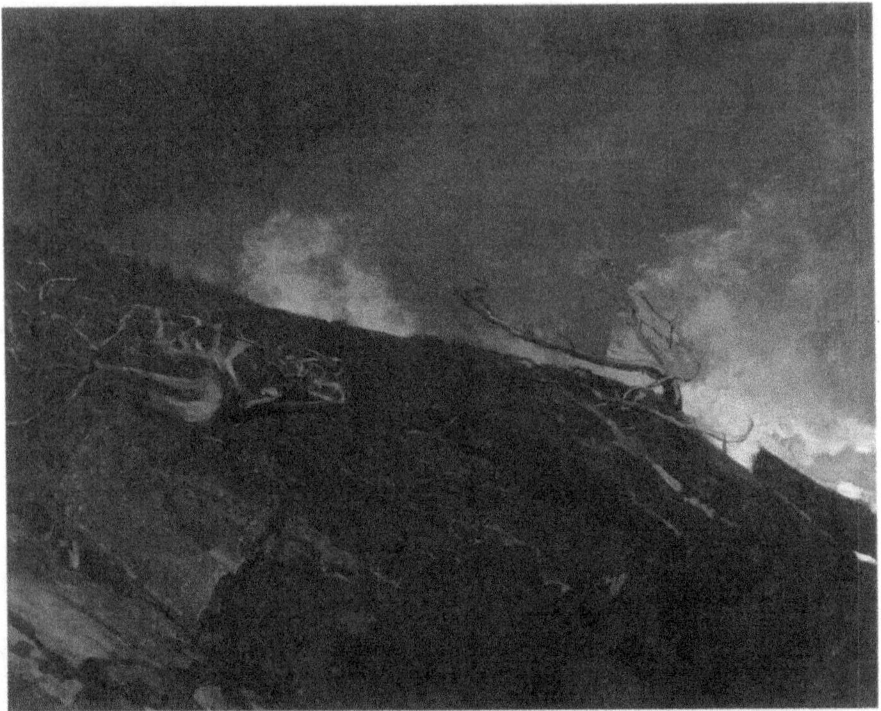

Figure 4.5 Winslow Homer, *Coast of Maine,* 1893.

The Art Institute of Chicago: Arthur Jerome Eddy Memorial Collection (1931.505).

to arrange for an exhibition of Whistler's recent work; however, the show did not take place. In the summer of 1897 Eddy offered to make travel arrangements for Whistler to come to the United States and to meet him in New York.[5] He gave several lectures about Whistler at the Art Institute of Chicago and at the Pennsylvania Academy in Philadelphia. After the artist's death in 1903, Eddy developed his memories into a book, *Recollections and Impressions of James A. McNeill Whistler,* in which he described Whistler's Paris studio at 86, rue Notre Dame des Champs. He explained how the artist had patiently worked on his portrait: "It was interesting to watch a picture grow under the hands of Whistler. With most painters something is finished from day to day, and in the course of ten or twelve sittings the portrait is complete. Not so with him. Nothing,

[5] "The Correspondence of James McNeill Whistler," Letter E15 dated July 16, 1897, accessed March 16, 2019, http://whistler.arts.gla.ac.uk/correspondence.

not a detail, not even an infinitesimal section of the background was finished until the last. He worked with great rapidity and long hours, but he used his colors thin and covered the canvas with innumerable coats of paint."[6] In *Recollections and Impressions*, Eddy described how the figure gradually emerged from the background and how, after the first few days, Whistler "would place the canvas in its frame, and thereafter paint with it so. ... He would paint all day from eleven in the morning until, well, until it was so dark that all was dim and shadowy and ghostly." [7] Sometimes they would have lunch together in the studio or go out to dinner at an unfrequented restaurant.

While in Paris Eddy purchased paintings from Durand-Ruel: Edouard Manet's *Beggar with Oysters (Philosopher)* (*Philosophe*) of 1865 (Figure 4.6) and *Portrait of Faure* (*Portrait de Faure*), as well as Claude Monet's *Snow Effect at Falaise* (*Effet de la neige à Falaise*) of 1886 (Figure 4.7). He also bought a painting of a girl by Auguste Renoir, but following Whistler's advice, returned it.[8] Durand-Ruel was well known because of its galleries in both Paris and New York. Bertha and Potter Palmer had acquired several paintings by Manet, Monet, and Renoir from the gallery in 1892. Eddy's selection of Impressionist paintings was not daring as these paintings were avidly collected in Chicago.

In Chicago in 1894, Robert Vonnoh painted portraits of Arthur Eddy's father (Figure 4.8), son (Figure 4.9), and wife, which he lent to the Art Institute in January 1896. Significantly, Eddy chose to have his own portrait painted in Paris by the expatriate Whistler and he became known in Chicago as "the man that Whistler painted."[9] Eddy was neither the first nor the only Chicago collector to purchase a work by Whistler: Bertha and Potter Palmer had acquired *Grey and Silver: Old Battersea Reach* in May 1892 and the Chicago banker John A. Lynch bought *Violet and Silver: The Deep Sea* in October 1894. In early December 1894, Paul Durand-Ruel had

---

[6] Arthur Jerome Eddy, *Recollections and Impressions of James A. McNeill Whistler* (Philadelphia: J. B. Lippincott, 1904), 235. The manuscript was completed September 16, 1903.

[7] Eddy, *Recollections and Impressions*, 242.

[8] "The Renoir I have *returned*—poor little girl, she never quite recovered from your very ungallant remarks." "The Correspondence of James McNeill Whistler," Letter E4 incorrectly dated, accessed March 16, 2019, http://whistler.arts.gla.ac.uk/correspondence.

[9] Quoted in Paul Kruty, "Arthur Jerome Eddy and His Collection: Prelude and Postscript to the Armory Show," *Arts Magazine* 61 (Feb. 1987): 40 without source and again in Liesl Olson, *Chicago Renaissance: Literature and Art in the Midwest Metropolis* (New Haven, CT: Yale University Press, 2017), 107.

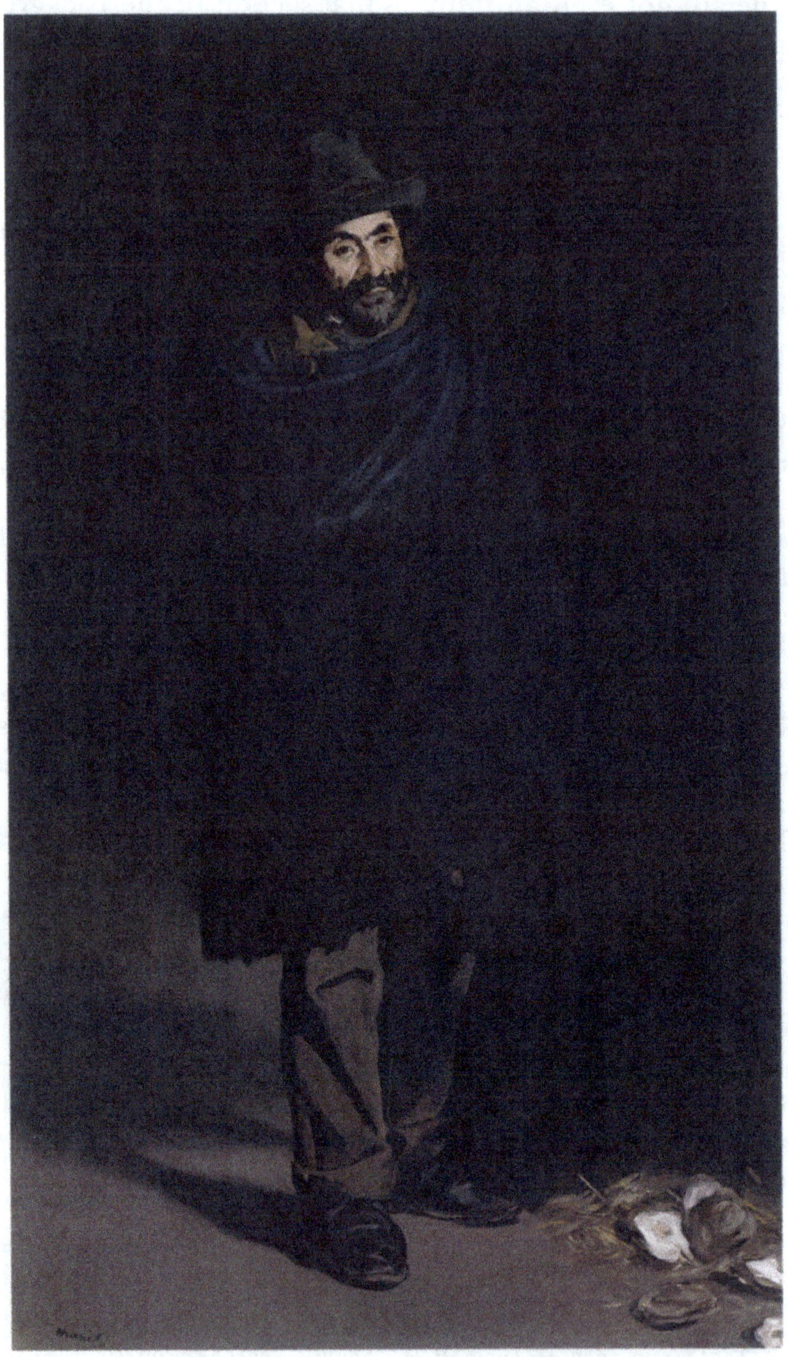

Figure 4.6 Edouard Manet, *Beggar with Oysters (Philosopher)*, 1865.
The Art Institute of Chicago: Arthur Jerome Eddy Memorial Collection (1931.504).

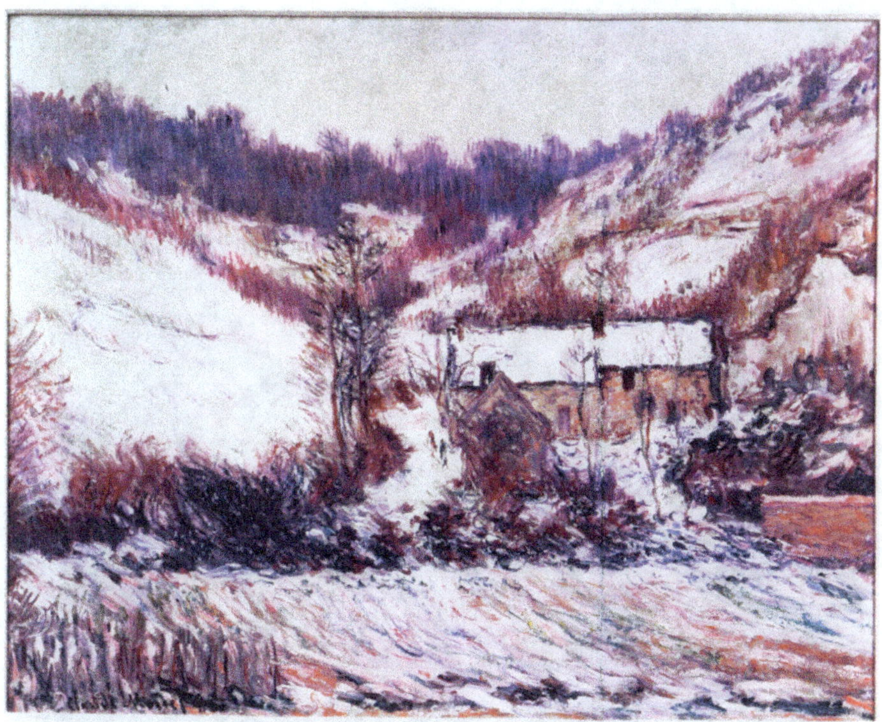

Figure 4.7 Claude Monet, *Snow Effect at Falaise*, 1886.

Private collection, Courtesy of Louis Stern Gallery, Los Angeles.

dinner with Arthur Eddy and John Lynch and admired this marine painting. The night before Durand-Ruel had dined with Eddy and was favorably impressed by his portrait.[10]

[10] "The Correspondence of James McNeill Whistler," Letter E7 dated December 5, 1894, accessed March 16, 2019, http://whistler.arts.gla.ac.uk/correspondence.

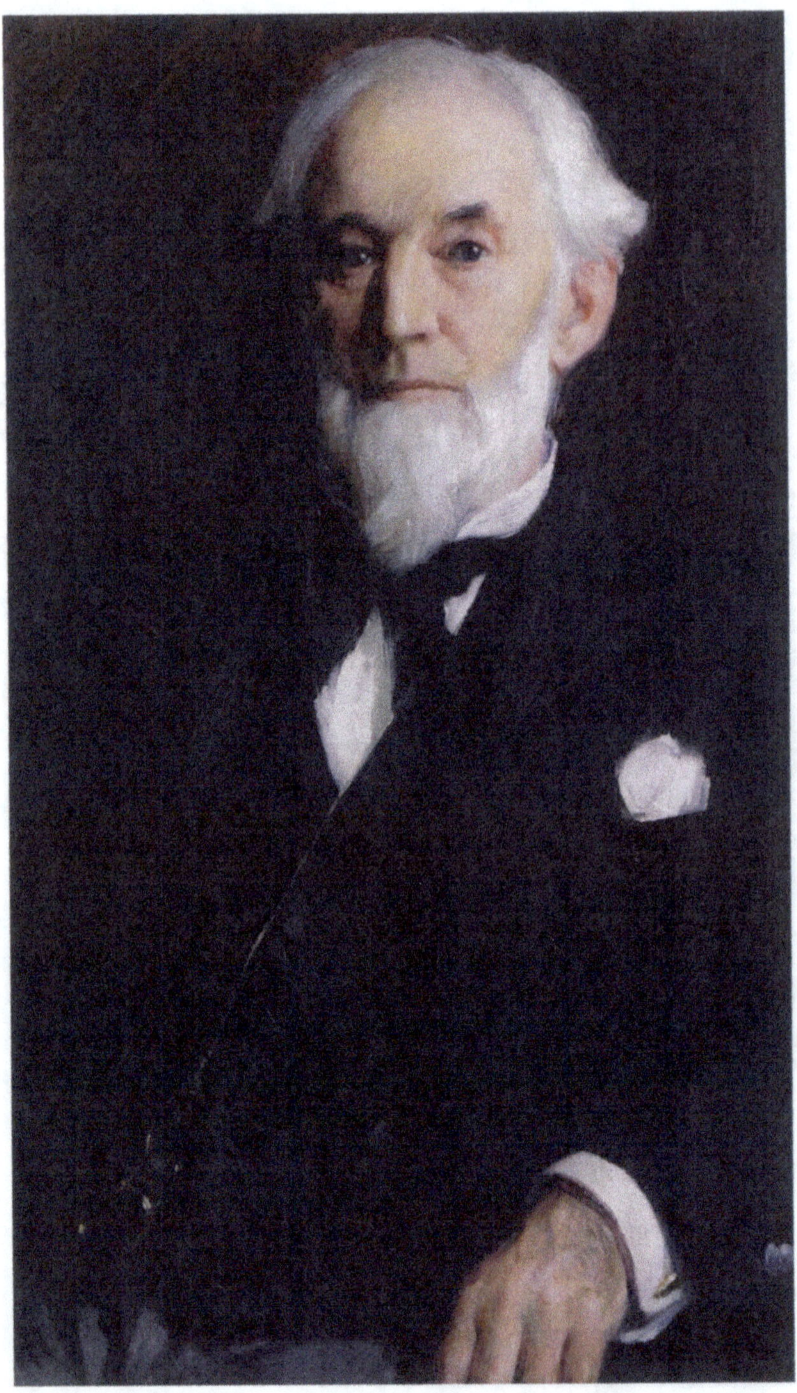

Figure 4.8 Robert Vonnoh, *Portrait of Jerome A. Eddy*, 1894.
Flint Institute of Arts, Flint, Michigan: Gift of Jerome O. Eddy (1940.3).

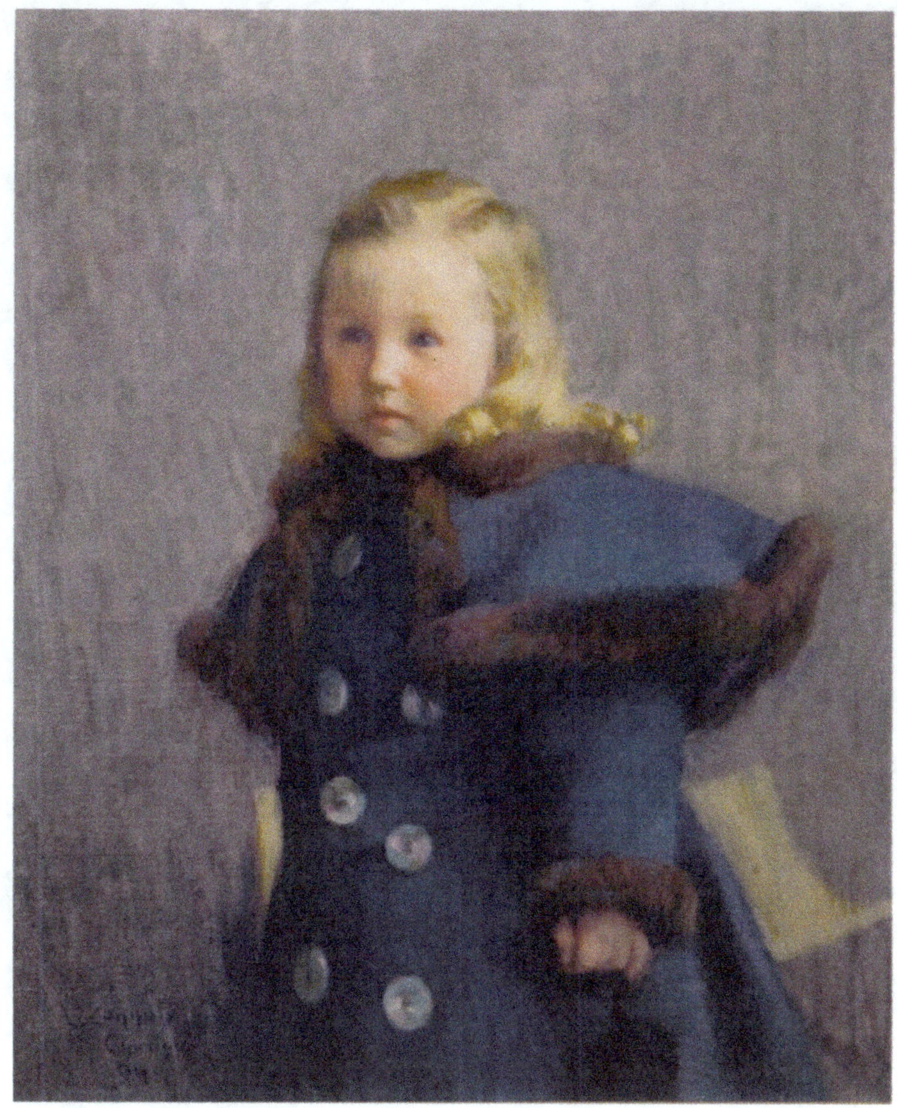

Figure 4.9 Robert Vonnoh, *Portrait of Jerome O. Eddy*, 1894.

Private collection, Chicago. Photograph courtesy of Madron Gallery.

# V

# Next Trip to Europe and Rodin, 1898

The Eddys went to Paris again in 1898. During this trip, Rodin made a sculpture of Arthur Jerome Eddy's likeness. Like Whistler, Rodin was popular among Chicago collectors. Bertha Palmer first visited Rodin's studio in June 1892 accompanied by Paul Durand-Ruel.[1] Charles T. Yerkes commissioned *Orpheus and Euridice* from Rodin in 1892 and the following year he acquired another marble, *Cupid and Psyche*.[2] In 1893, Mrs. Addie M. Hall Ellis gave a Rodin plaster to the Art Institute, where it was exhibited as *Citizen of Calais* in December when the Institute's new building opened.[3] Robert Allerton also owned a Rodin bronze of a *Caryatid* from c. 1891, which he gave to the Art Institute along with other bronzes.[4] According to the society pages of the *Chicago Daily Tribune*, Mr. and Mrs. Arthur J. Eddy sailed on the *Fürst Bismarck* on July 28, 1898.[5] He was back in Chicago on September 19, 1898. In a letter to William M. R. French, the Art Institute's director, Eddy wrote: "While in Paris I spent several days with Rodin watching him at work and conversing with him; in fact, I had exceptional facilities for becoming acquainted with him, and becoming familiar with his ideas. I think I will attempt only one lecture this year and that will be on Rodin. You may call it 'Hours with Rodin,' and the lecture can be illustrated with a stereoptican. Rodin loaned me some twenty or more photographs of his most important works."[6]

*Bust of Arthur Jerome Eddy* (*Buste d'homme* [M. Eddy]; Figure 5.1) bears the date 1898, which, together with the absence of a foundry mark, suggests that it was the first cast.[7] An invoice from Griffoul et Lorge dated October 29, 1898, indicates when the casting took place. Moreover, work on the sculpture must have been completed

---

[1] Anna Tahinci, "Rodin and His American Collectors," in *Rodin and America: Influence and Adaptation, 1876–1936*, exh. cat. (Iris & B. Gerald Cantor Center for Visual Arts at Stanford University, 2011), 317–18.

[2] Both sculptures now belong to the Metropolitan Museum of Art (10.63.1 and 10.63.2).

[3] *Catalogue of Paintings, Sculpture, and Other Objects Exhibited at the Opening of the New Museum*, no. 417. This bronze-painted plaster (1893.187) was the first work by Rodin to be acquired by an American museum.

[4] See Art Institute of Chicago accession numbers 1924.5, 1924.813, and 1923.1.

[5] "Events in Chicago Society," *Chicago Daily Tribune*, July 29, 1898, 8. Passenger lists for the *Fürst Bismarck* are not available. The ship belonged to the Hamburg–American Line and stopped in Southampton on the way to Germany.

[6] Letter dated September 20, 1898, from Eddy to W. M. R. French, William M. R. French Papers in the Archives of the Art Institute.

[7] Antoinette Le Normand-Romain, *The Bronzes of Rodin: Catalogue of Works in the Musée Rodin* (Paris: Editions de la Réunion des Musées Nationaux, 2007), vol. I, 316–17. The bronze was cast by Auguste Griffoul in 1898.

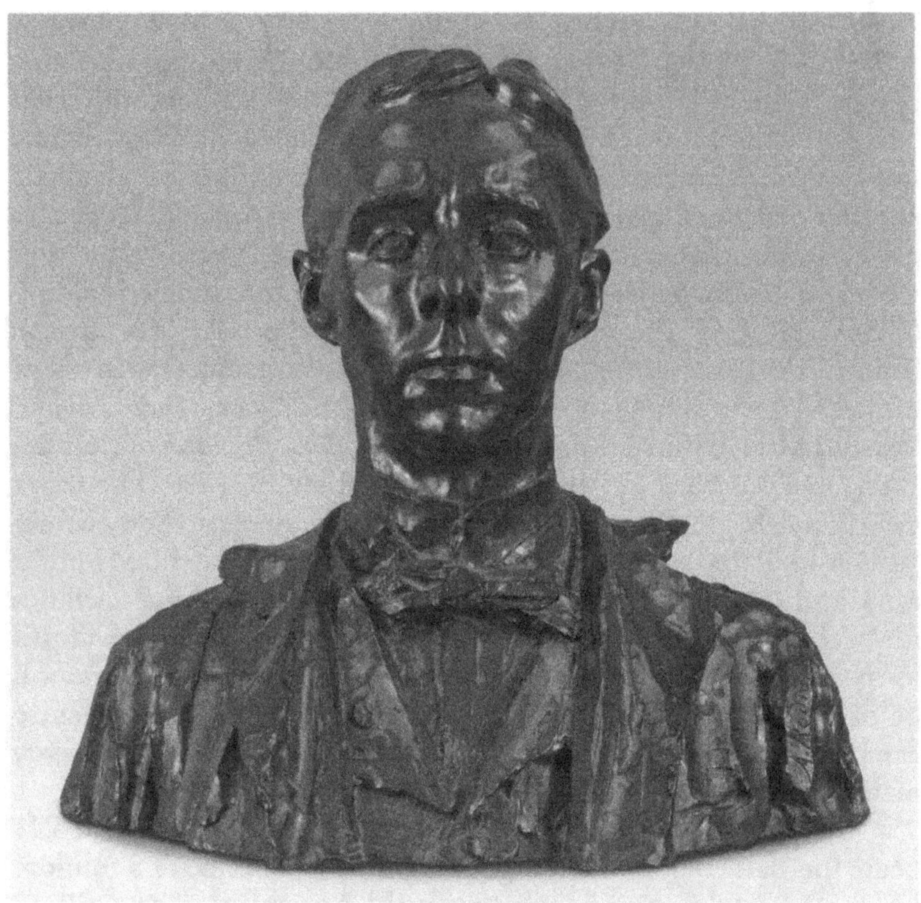

Figure 5.1 Auguste Rodin, *Bust of Arthur Jerome Eddy*, 1898.

The Art Institute of Chicago: Arthur Jerome Eddy Memorial Collection (1931.502).

at least two months earlier.[8] In early correspondence the sculpture is referred to as the "portrait of the American."[9] Eddy paid Rodin 8,000 francs for the bronze and the original plaster of the bust. In the same letter, dated December 30, 1898, he told Rodin that, "if you need to keep the bust and exhibit it in the spring, you are free to do so" (*si vous avez soin de conserver le buste et de l'exposer au printemps,*

[8] Information regarding the time required for posing, preparation for casting, and finishing the bronze was kindly provided by Jérôme Le Blay in correspondence, May 16, 2019.

[9] Letter from A. Griffoul & Cie., 26 rue au Maire to Rodin dated October 29, 1898, Musée Rodin, Paris.

*vous êtes libre de le faire*). He also wanted to know what had become of the original plaster and inquired about a small bronze head resembling a mask, which was in the atelier, that he would be happy to buy for six hundred francs if it were still available, and he suggested that the artist send it with the bust.[10] When Eddy was in Paris again in October 1899 he stopped at Rodin's studio before leaving for Dieppe, but the sculptor was not there. He wrote to say he "was very sorry to leave Paris without seeing more of you" and enclosed an announcement of his talk at the Art Institute of Chicago on December 12, 1899.[11] His lecture was titled "Hours with Rodin" in contrast to "Days with Whistler" almost two years earlier. Although the time he may have spent posing for Rodin was brief, Eddy stayed in contact with the artist until 1913.

In April 1900 Eddy had the bronze shipped back to Rodin, who exhibited it in his retrospective at the Pavillon de l'Alma. Rodin told him that: "Your bust [is] well-placed in my exhibition and gives a very good impression." (*Votre buste figure en bonne place à mon exposition et produit un très bon effet.*)[12] In his correspondence concerning the return shipment, Eddy specified that a certificate from the American consulate must state that the work had been sent to France as a loan and was to be returned in bond so he would not have to pay duty at customs. At an unspecified date probably in 1899, Eddy acquired the *Man with Broken Nose* (*L'Homme au nez cassé*), created in 1864, to which he had referred in his letter of December 30, 1898. In the same letter he wrote that, "it will be necessary to advise the shippers to prepare the necessary declarations for the little bronze separate from those for the bust." ([*I*]*l sera nécessaire de les en aviser et de faire les déclarations nécessaires à propos du petit bronze. Les papiers consulaires concernant le petit bronze devront être séparés de ceux concernant le buste.*) In 1931, Eddy's widow and son donated the *Man with Broken Nose* and the *Bust of Arthur Jerome Eddy* to the Art Institute.

The whereabouts of the original plaster for the Eddy bust arose again when the artist wanted to have more casts made. In October 1912, Eddy found that he did in fact have the plaster in an unopened

[10] Letter in French dated December 30, 1898, from Eddy to Rodin, belongs to the Musée Rodin.

[11] Letter in English dated October 26, 1899, from Eddy to Rodin as well as other correspondence is preserved in the Archives of the Musée Rodin, Paris. Rodin's letters to Eddy are lost.

[12] Alain Beausire and Florence Cadouot, eds., *Correspondance de Rodin* (Paris: Musée Rodin, 1986), vol. II, 30.

crate and told Rodin: "Since I wrote you, I found the original plaster of the bust and I will send it to you in place of the bronze. American law would make me pay tax if I sent the original bronze a second time." (*Depuis que J'ai vous ecrit J'ai trouve l'original platre du buste et Je vous enverrez le platre en place du bronze. La loi Americaine me ferait paye empot pour le second fois si J'envoyais l'original bronze.*)[13] Always the lawyer, he fought the imposition of duties and tariffs, especially on works of art.

Eddy mentioned Rodin in *Delight, the Soul of Art; Five Lectures,* which was published in October 1902: "In the controversy which raged in France over Rodin's 'Balzac,' the vast majority of those who participated seemed to lose sight of the fact that the value of the work lay not in any real or supposed likeness to Balzac,—that is a matter of comparative indifference,—but in the fact that the heroic figure was and is Rodin's conception of Balzac,—a genius's conception of a genius,—and as such is of infinitely greater worth than any number of more faithful likenesses by lesser men."[14] The controversy surrounding Rodin's *Balzac* occurred in 1898, the same year that Eddy met the sculptor in Paris.

Among the artist's papers at the Musée Rodin, there is a photograph of Arthur Jerome Eddy taken by the Chicago photographer William Koehne (Figure 5.2), which bears such an uncanny resemblance to the sculpture (see Figure 5.1) that one can only surmise that Rodin worked primarily from the photograph. The sitter's facial features, the way his hair is parted, the bow tie, collar, vest, and jacket lapels are the same in both the photograph and the bronze: In the sculpture, the pose is more frontal, the shoulders are squared, and the hands are omitted. Close examination of the photograph raises certain questions: the dedication and date inscribed on the back of the photo, October 20, 1900, is, however, later than that on the sculpture. Moreover, Eddy was certainly not in Paris at that time. In addition, the stamp on the photograph, "Koehne/Huron & Clark Streets/Chicago," is appropriate for 1900, but not 1898. William L. Koehne was from Texas; he worked with Charles F. Bretzman, who was born in Hannover, Germany, and lived in Chicago from 1894–1900. In 1898, photographs from their studio bear the stamp of Koehne and Bretzman, but by 1900 only the name of Koehne

[13] Letter dated October 17, 1912, from Eddy to Rodin, belongs to the Musée Rodin, Paris.
[14] Arthur Jerome Eddy, *Delight, the Soul of Art; Five Lectures* (Philadelphia: J. B. Lippincott, 1902), 103. The sculpture of Balzac was commissioned in 1891, but was only completed in March 1898.

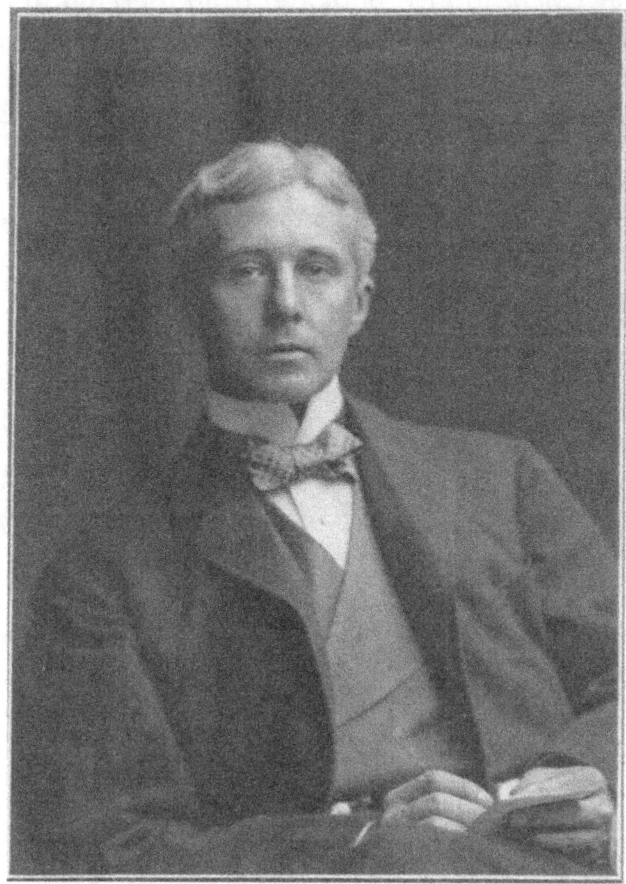

Figure 5.2 William Koehne, *Photograph of Arthur Jerome Eddy*, 1900.
Image courtesy of Musée Rodin, Paris.

appears. It is possible that Eddy sent a new print of the photo to the sculptor when the bronze was exhibited at the Pavillon de l'Alma. Given Rodin's close working relationship with photographers and the large number of photographs he amassed,[15] the hypothesis that he relied on Koehne's photograph seems plausible.

From Eddy's letters to Rodin, we know that he went to Europe in 1899 and 1903. Moreover, in 1899 the collector wrote Whistler that he and Mrs. Eddy would sail on August 15 on the White Star

[15] See Hélène Pinet, ed., *Rodin et la photographie*, exh. cat. (Paris: Musée Rodin, 2007). Among immense holdings in the Archives of the Musée Rodin, about 7,000 photographs were assembled by the sculptor between 1877 and 1917.

Line steamer *Cymric* to Liverpool and from there go to Glasgow to see the portrait of Carlyle before spending a few days in London and then continuing to Paris, where they would stay at The Chatham.[16] Eddy stayed again at the Hotel Chatham in rue Dounou in April 1903.

[16] "The Correspondence of James McNeill Whistler," Letter E18 dated August 10, 1899, accessed March 16, 2019, http://whistler.arts.gla.ac.uk/correspondence.

# VI

## *Delight, the Soul of Art; Five Lectures; Two Thousand Miles on an Automobile*, 1902

In the late 1890s, Arthur Eddy lectured frequently on a wide range of subjects. He was a Gold Democrat active in the Iroquois Club: He spoke at an Illinois State Bar Association banquet, was elected Vice-President of the Chicago Bar Association, became President of the Iroquois Club, and participated in numerous debates. The offices of Walker & Eddy moved from The Rookery to 800 The Temple, an even newer and taller building also by the architectural firm Burnham and Root. Not only did he speak about his "Days with Whistler" and his "Hours with Rodin," but Eddy gave lectures at the Art Institute on "Standards in Art and Literature," "Thought—The Mind of Art," and "The Lost Sense of the Beautiful." Somehow he found time to write. An article on Edouard Manet illustrating the two paintings Eddy owned (and expressing his opinions on the merits of other works) was published in *Brush and Pencil* in February 1898. In the autumn of 1899, Eddy wrote a text on the Boer War that Whistler had sent to Théodore Duret: It appeared as "*Le conflit anglo-Boer au point de vue du droit*" translated by Francis Vielé-Griffin in *Mercure de France* in 1900.[1] In 1901 Eddy published *The Law of Combinations: Embracing Monopolies, Trusts and Combinations of Labor and Capital, Conspiracy, and Contracts in Restraint of Trade*[2] and, the following year, *Delight, the Soul of Art; Five Lectures.*

Completed in November 1900, *The Law of Combinations* is dedicated to a lawyer from Ohio, Samuel E. Williamson, General Counsel of the New York Central and Hudson River Railroad. On the title page, Eddy identifies himself as a member of the Chicago Bar. The two-volume treatise presents in detail federal and state legislation pertaining to monopolies, corporations, conspiracies, and anti-trust laws. He considers *combinations* to be economic factors in the industrial and commercial world, a fact with which legislatures struggle and often do not recognize. He views common law as a "noble development" better able to deal with the evolution of economic conditions "than laws which are arbitrary and frequently the thoughtless edicts of man."[3] Eddy provides definitions and gives

[1] F. V-G., "Le conflit anglo-Boer au point de vue du droit," *Mercure de France* 34 (April–June 1900): 131–48.

[2] Arthur J. Eddy, *The Law of Combinations: Embracing Monopolies, Trusts, and Combinations of Labor and Capital; Conspiracy, and Contracts in Restraint of Trade Together with Federal and State Anti-trust Legislation and the Incorporation Laws of New Jersey, West Virginia and Delaware* (Chicago: Callaghan and Company, 1901), 2 vols. It was reviewed in the *Harvard Law Review* in March 1901 and in the *Yale Law Journal* in April 1901.

[3] Eddy, *Law of Combinations*, vol. 1, vi.

historical references for monopolies; he defines *combinations* as "the co-operation of two or more persons to achieve a given result" and distinguishes between legal and illegal combinations.[4] There is a lengthy index of cases cited and there are extensive footnotes. He does not hesitate to interject his opinions especially in discussing remedies and in drawing conclusions. Eddy states that: "Social progress would be impossible were it not for co-operation and combination; therefore the law recognizes and encourages the formation of 1) Partnerships, 2) Voluntary associations, and 3) Corporations. Law frequently permits and sometimes expressly authorizes consolidation of partnerships and of corporations. All of which are combinations of combinations."[5]

In contrast, in *Delight, the Soul of Art,* Eddy investigates the eternal question: "What is art? The question is as old as man himself, for we have no records of men without some manifestation of the art-impulse; and it is a question that has been answered in as many different ways as there are different minds."[6] For Eddy, art is delight in thought and symbol. Thought strives to express itself and symbol is the means whereby it achieves that end: "art is the delight in both the thought and the symbol. Without the double delight,—the combination of these two quite distinct delights,—there can be no art."[7] In discussing the soul of art, he refers to the Aborigines in Australia, the Sistine Chapel in Rome, the *Nike of Samothrace* in the Louvre. He analyzes three essential elements that enter into the production of a work of art (the spiritual element—Delight, the subjective element—Thought or Conception, the objective element—Symbol or Expression), citing Franz Hals and Rembrandt van Rijn and praising the work of Diego Velazquez.[8] When considering sincerity and conviction, he focuses on the art of Jean François Millet and Whistler; however, the chapter on inspiration turns to literature and specifically John Milton and Ralph Waldo Emerson. Likewise, the essay on expression brings in the writings of Elizabeth Browning, Alfred Tennyson, Walt Whitman, and William Shakespeare after mentioning paintings by Vasily Vereshchagin, Peter Paul Rubens, J. M. W. Turner, and Monet. In the final chapter on "Delight

[4] Eddy, *Law of Combinations,* vol. 1, 115–17.
[5] Eddy, *Law of Combinations,* vol. 2, 1327.
[6] Arthur Jerome Eddy, *Delight, the Soul of Art; Five Lectures* (Philadelphia: J. B. Lippincott, 1902), 9.
[7] Eddy, *Delight,* 10.
[8] Eddy, *Delight,* 52–58.

in Labor," Eddy concedes that the meaning of art is hard to define, but posits that true art is the product of the human soul, whereas pseudo-art is mechanically produced factory art. Within this context he describes how Whistler makes his lithographs and praises Japanese prints.[9] More than a century ago, he lamented:

> Ours is the age of commercialism and industrialism, of production for trade rather than for pleasure. Men "collect" nowadays; they do not hunt for and acquire this or that beautiful work of art for the pleasure it is going to give them and their children from generation to generation,—not at all; pictures are bought as investments, porcelains as speculations, books for their bindings,—the commercial instinct dominates.[10]

Yet he saw signs that Americans were tiring of industrialism and that handwork was coming into fashion.

In 1900 Arthur Eddy obtained a driver's license, took part in the first run of the Automobile Club in Chicago (of which he was president), and attended the auto show held under the auspices of the Automobile Club of America at Madison Square Garden in New York (where he sat at the speakers' table). On August 1, 1901, Mr. and Mrs. Eddy set out from their home in Chicago[11] and drove to New England and back via New York, Canada, and Michigan. On August 30 he was charged with speeding and fined in Pittsfield, Massachusetts.[12] Not only did they travel 2,900 miles in his car but Eddy also wrote a book about the adventure under the pseudonym "chauffeur," *Two Thousand Miles on an Automobile; Being a Desultory Narrative of a Trip through New England, New York, Canada, and the West.* He describes in detail the roads, towns, and people encountered along the way, as well as mishaps such as breaking down and not having a mechanic. The book is dedicated to his wife, "who for more than sixteen hundred miles of the journey faced dangers and discomforts with an equanimity worthy a better cause"; it includes eighteen illustrations by Frank Verbeck. As was his nature, the author expresses his opinion on most everything from what to wear while automobiling, to what and how to drive, as well as advice on how

---

[9] Eddy, *Delight*, 248–57.

[10] Eddy, *Delight*, 284.

[11] On October 1, 1896, Eddy bought a three-story house at 1635 Sheridan Road from Loretta B. James and Frederick S. James. He and his wife lived in Buena Park on the north side for the rest of their lives.

[12] *Chicago Daily Tribune*, September 1, 1901, 3.

to meet the challenges. His car was "an ordinary twelve hundred dollar single cylinder American machine" with eight and a half horsepower.[13] Upon returning from the sixty-day trip, he related that, "taken as a whole, no more interesting and delightful trip could be imagined. Mr. Eddy was not accompanied by an expert machinist or chauffeur and he had to face unaided whatever critical moments were encountered on the trip."[14]

Arthur Eddy was, of course, neither a chauffeur, nor a critic, but a corporation lawyer. By 1901 he was a partner with Patrick C. Haley and Charles A. Munroe in Eddy, Haley & Munroe, with offices at 800 The Temple. Eddy and Haley argued cases in the Appellate Division and in the Northern District of the Illinois Supreme Court. They represented Mrs. Helen M. Gardner in a case about a mortgage in the Appellate Court in 1900 and again in the Supreme Court (*Gardner et al. v. Cohn et al.*) the following year. In 1902 they argued for the plaintiff in a case involving a railroad company (*Wells v. Northern Trust Company et al.*) in the Supreme Court of Illinois and they successfully represented the appellants in *Arnold et al. v. Northwestern Telephone Company* in the same court.

At the beginning of the twentieth century, Eddy's interests, as chronicled in the newspapers, ranged from cars to politics, from taxation to litigation, from strikes to the visit of Prince Henry of Prussia, from music to architecture and, of course, art. By 1900 he owned at least fourteen works of art by American and French artists. In December 1903 he expanded the scope of his collecting by purchasing four Japanese scrolls from Yamanaka and Company in New York.[15] He also owned a Japanese print by Hiroshige, although which work and the date he bought it remain unknown. Eddy acquired a painting, *Girl in Pink*, by Frederick Carl Frieseke (Figure 6.1) in early 1904 at the time of the 73rd Annual Exhibition at the Pennsylvania Academy of Fine Arts.[16] Although the picture may not

---

[13] "Chauffeur," *Two Thousand Miles on an Automobile; Being a Desultory Narrative of a Trip through New England, New York, Canada, and the West* (Philadelphia: J. B. Lippincott, 1902), 20.

[14] "America Cup in Danger," *Chicago Daily Tribune*, October 1, 1901, 12.

[15] A letter dated April 12, 1937, from his daughter-in-law, Effie Eddy, to the art dealer Earl Stendahl states that "yesterday I came across the original receipt from Yamanaka and Company, New York dated December 11th, 1903 for the old Kakemonos you have." Stendahl Art Galleries Records, Archives of American Art, Smithsonian Institution, Washington DC, Reel 2717. Stendahl sold the works to a California collector; they have not been identified further.

[16] A letter dated March 25, 1904, from Frieseke to Sarah O'Bryan, indicates that, "my picture was bought by a Mr. Eddy of Chicago who has a fine collection—Whistlers and things." Letter in the Frieseke Family Archive kindly brought to my attention by Nicholas Kilmer in correspondence, January 24, 2011.

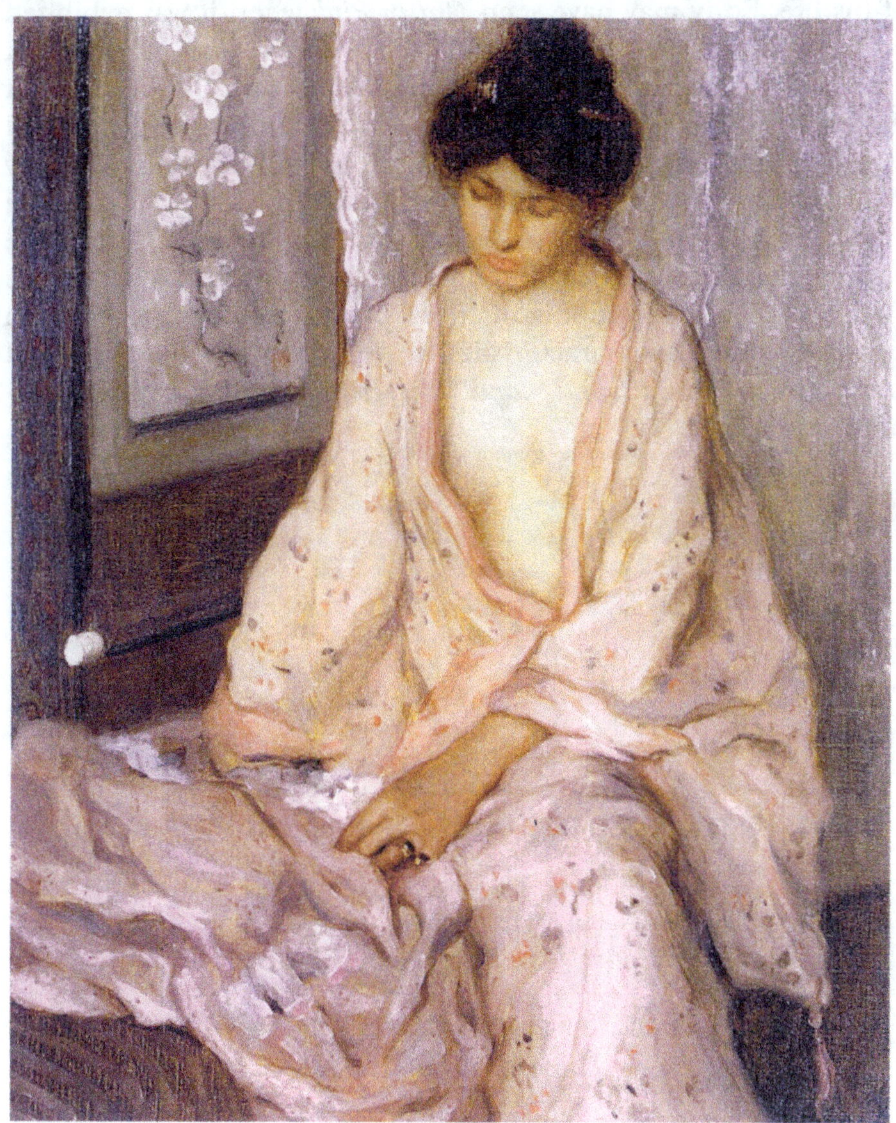

Figure 6.1 Frederick Carl Frieseke, *Girl in Pink*, 1903.

Private collection.

resemble earlier purchases, there are reasons why Eddy might have noticed the artist. Frieseke was born in Michigan in 1874, took classes at the Art Institute of Chicago, studied in Paris at the Académie Julian, and then with Whistler at the Académie Carmen. He is considered an American Impressionist who lived in France much of his life. Eddy may have seen *Girl in Pink* when it was exhibited in the Salon in Paris in April 1903 (as *Femme en rose*) or later that year in the 16th Annual Exhibition of American Oil Paintings at the Art Institute. The delicate colors and tranquil scene of a model seated in an interior bring to mind paintings by Manet and especially Whistler. It can also be related to the early portrait of Eddy (see Figure 2.1), Vonnoh's portrait of his son (see Figure 4.9), and one of the first paintings he acquired, *Hagar and Ishmael* by Walker (see Figure 4.4). The prettiness of these paintings contrasts with the vigorous, muscular characteristics of American art that he would later praise in *Cubists and Post-Impressionism*[17] as "Virile-Impressionism."

[17] Arthur Jerome Eddy, *Cubists and Post-Impressionism* (Chicago: A. C. McClurg & Co., 1914).

# VII

## Pasadena, His House, Friends, and Fishing, 1905–07

In February 1902 Mrs. Eddy traveled to Pasadena; while there she stayed at the Raymond Hotel.[1] Later that year in December, she again traveled to California to stay for the winter while her husband was planning a trip to Greece to study ancient art and, through Prince Henry of Prussia whom he had met earlier that year, made contact with German archeologists. Arthur Eddy sailed to Cherbourg on the *Deutschland* on January 28, 1903, attended a court ball in Berlin at the invitation of Kaiser Wilhelm in February, saw Rodin in Paris in April, and arrived back in New York on the same ship on May 1, 1903.

It did not take long before Eddy was enchanted with southern California. He bought land on Euclid Avenue in Pasadena in April 1905 and had a house built that was modeled on native Mexican and Spanish dwellings. An article published in *The Craftsman* in November 1906 states that "the owner employed no architect and depended on no tradition beyond his own recognition of the completeness with which the old adobe houses had met and fulfilled every condition of climate, surroundings and the life that was lived in them."[2] An article in *International Studio* reiterates that "Mr. Eddy planned and designed his own house, even the details of the furniture and metal work."[3] However, Robert Winter convincingly analyzed the blueprints (floor plan and elevation) now at Occidental College in Pasadena, and proved that the architect was, in fact, Frederick Louis Roehrig, who designed the Green Hotel and several homes in Pasadena.[4]

Although no author is listed for the first article in *The Craftsman*, the views expressed are clearly those of Eddy. The text begins: "Arthur Jerome Eddy, in writing to a friend his views on the building of dwelling-houses, once said: 'Generally speaking, all native built dwellings are useful and appropriate, and therefore entirely harmonious with their settings, whereas, generally speaking, most architecturally built dwellings are neither very useful nor very appropriate, and do not harmonize with their settings.'" Mr. Eddy apologized for not having time to write the article as requested, but he sent

[1] "Mrs. George M. Pullman Offers Golf Trophy in Pasadena," *Chicago Daily Tribune*, February 28, 1902, 16.

[2] "A California House Modeled on the Simple Lines of the Old Mission Dwelling: Hence Meeting All Requirements of Climate and Environment," *The Craftsman* XI, no. 2 (November 1906): 208.

[3] Florence Williams, "The Southern California Bungalow—A Local Problem in Housing," *International Studio* 30, no. 120 (February 1907): lxxvii.

[4] Robert Winter, *The California Bungalow* (Santa Monica, CA: Hennessey and Ingalls, 1980), 40–41.

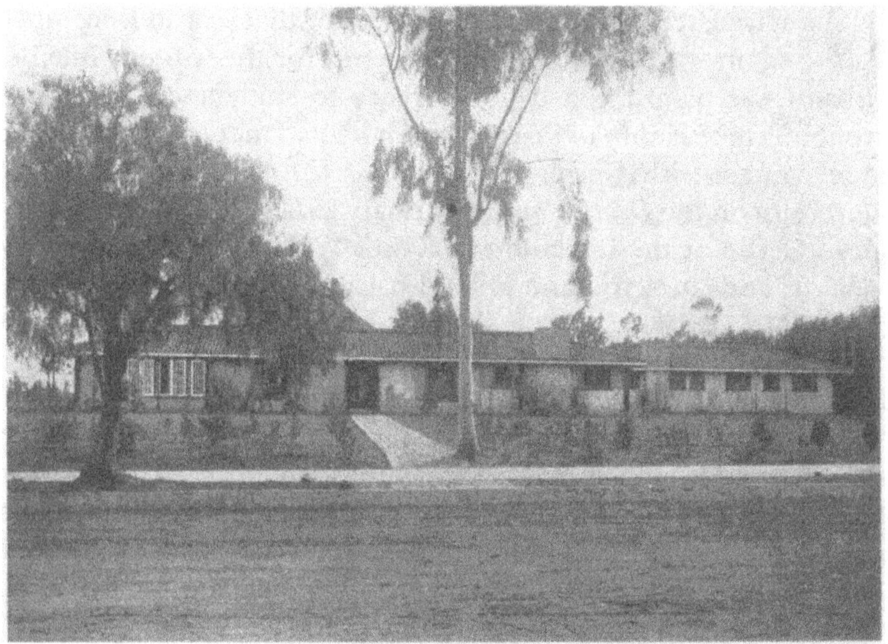

Figure 7.1 Exterior of A. J. Eddy's Bungalow in Pasadena, *The Craftsman* (November 1906): 209.

University of Wisconsin–Madison Libraries, Digital Library for the Decorative Arts and Material Culture.

photographs to accompany the anonymous text.[5] However, he authored the second article, which appeared in the May 1907 issue of *The Craftsman.*[6] This essay focused on tiled roofs and contained detailed analysis of building methods.

From studying the photographs of the house that appeared in *The Craftsman,* we know what the exterior (Figure 7.1) and interior (Figure 7.2) of the house looked like as well as the lamps credited to Eddy (Figure 7.3), and the simple furnishings he selected. The house in Pasadena no longer exists and, like his home in Buena Park in Chicago, was demolished to make way for a modern apartment building. The architectural style of each Eddy home as well as the artworks on view were distinct and totally different: The

[5] *The Craftsman,* XI, no. 2 (November 1906): 208–21.

[6] Arthur Jerome Eddy, "Tiled Roofs: The Kind of Buildings to Which They Are Suited and a Method of Construction that Makes Them Practical as Well as Picturesque," *The Craftsman* XII, no. 2 (May 1907): 180–92. Eddy had published a short text, "Sincerity in Art," in *The Craftsman* IX (October 1905): 22.

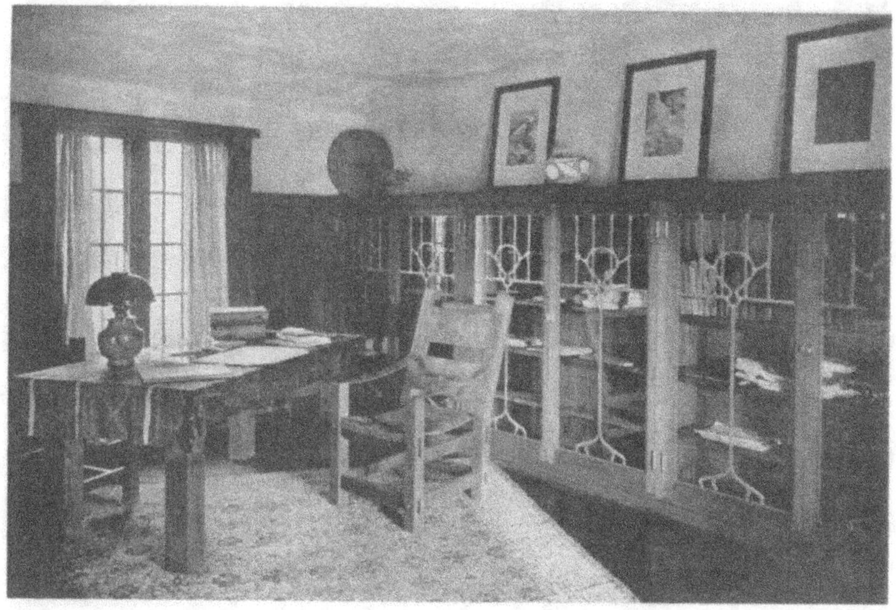

Figure 7.2 View of Eddy's study in Pasadena bungalow, *The Craftsman* (November 1906): 221.

University of Wisconsin–Madison Libraries, Digital Library for the Decorative Arts and Material Culture.

painting by Frieseke (see Figure 6.1) would never have been shown in the Pasadena house and the lamps and Native American artifacts seen in the dining room in California would not have been displayed in Chicago. Although Eddy may well have designed the lamps and proposed the courtyard, it is impossible that someone without architectural training would have been able to drawn up such precise plans for the Mission-style bungalow, with its interior courtyard and distinctive architectural details.

In the autumn of 1906, Stirling and Nanette Calder moved with their young son, Alexander, to Euclid Avenue in Pasadena. A family of artists, they lived down the street from the Eddys, were fascinated with the arts and crafts of the Southwest, collected baskets and jewelry, and even had the same kind of wicker chairs as the Eddys.[7] Arthur Eddy commissioned Nanette Calder to paint his wife's portrait (which was exhibited at the Art Institute of Chicago

[7] Jed Perl, *Calder: The Conquest of Time. The Early Years, 1898–1940* (New York: Alfred A. Knopf, 2017), 68.

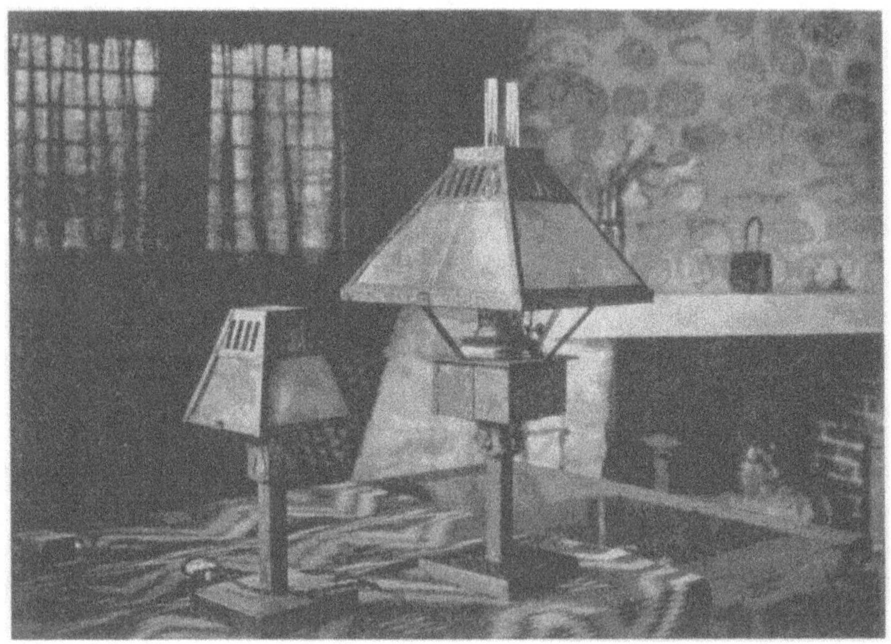

Figure 7.3 Electric lamps of hammered iron and mica designed by Eddy for Pasadena home, *The Craftsman* (November 1906), 217.

University of Wisconsin–Madison Libraries, Digital Library for the Decorative Arts and Material Culture.

in 1912). The whereabouts of the portrait are unknown, but the 1920 inventory of Arthur Eddy's estate lists it as "Figure in Riding Habit" and gives a date of 1907. Decades later Alexander Calder recalled that his parents could not understand why Eddy never bought any of Stirling's sculptures. He remembered that when he was about nine years old Eddy encouraged him to exercise by signing him up for a course at Maloney's gym, making him swim, and getting him a bicycle.[8]

Soon after the turn of the century, the society columns of the *Chicago Daily Tribune* were filled with reports of people who went to Pasadena for the winter. Chicagoans who stayed in Pasadena included Carter H. Harrison,[9] Samuel W. Allerton, George M. Pull-

[8] Alexander Calder with Jean Davidson, *Calder: An Autobiography with Pictures* (Boston: Beacon Press, 1966), 25. Dictated January 16, 1965.

[9] Carter H. Harrison, *Growing Up with Chicago: Sequel to "Stormy Years"* (Chicago: Ralph Fletcher Seymour, 1944), 196.

man, members of the Armour family, Chauncey J. Blair, Richard T. Crane, Henry C. Durand, Otho S. A. Sprague, and later John Wrigley, Jr. The Eddys belonged to the Valley Hunt Club. From 1905 to 1909 the names of both Mr. and Mrs. Eddy were mentioned in the *Pasadena Daily News* and the *Los Angeles Times.* Mrs. Eddy hosted luncheons and poured tea at card parties and receptions. Arthur Eddy's name appeared most often within the context of fishing on Catalina Island.

As early as May 1, 1905, Eddy offered a silver cup for the largest yellow tail caught with light tackle at the Santa Catalina Tuna Club. In April 1906 he founded the Catalina Light Tackle Club and that summer established a silver cup for the largest gold button fish. Eddy also wrote a series of eleven articles on "Light Tackle Sea Fishing" that were published in the magazine *Forest and Stream* during the summer of 1907.[10] Later that year he traveled to New York for a meeting at the Natural History Museum to organize a national anglers club. His activities in California were not limited to fishing; they also included refereeing a fencing match at Maloney's gym in Pasadena, attending the opera, and giving a lecture on Whistler at the Valley Hunt Club.

Eddy was an enthusiastic advocate of fencing. In 1906 he arranged for James Murray, Jr., a well-known instructor at the New York Athletic Club, to come to Pasadena for the summer to take charge of fencing classes at H. W. Maloney's gymnasium on West Green Street.[11] Maloney was president of the Pasadena Fencers Club. In Pasadena on April 20, 1907, Eddy, assisted by Prof. Alberti of Los Angeles and H. C. Berls of New York, judged several competitions, and the other two gave a demonstration with broadswords.[12] He established Eddy cups at the Los Angeles Athletic Club and the Fencers' Club in New York. The society columnist for the *Chicago Daily Tribune* wrote: "Our old friend Arthur J. Eddy, the art connoisseur, the collector of fine books, the fancier of choice vintages, the pioneer of motoring, the novelist, playwright, and modern Isaak Walton, has added a new leaf to his wreath of laurels. He never does anything by halves and has for some time been devoting himself

[10] See *Forest and Stream,* LXVIII, no. 22, 858–59; no. 23, 898–99; no. 24, 939–40; no. 25, 977; no. 26, 1016–17; LXIX, no. 1, 18–19; no. 2, 59–60; no. 3, 97–98; no. 4, 137–38; no. 5, 176–77; no. 6, 218–19.

[11] *Pasadena Daily News,* June 21, 1906, 9.

[12] See *Los Angeles Times,* April 20, 1907, II10 and April 21, 1907, 18.

to fencing ... There is this to be said—and it is not fear of his sword that impels me to say it—that whatever Arthur Eddy undertakes he does well and generally better than the next man."[13] In 1913 the same newspaper reported that Eddy, who was "internationally famous as a fencer," spoke to the Woman's Club about the art of fencing. "[He] told of bouts he had enjoyed with the swordsmen of Paris and the swordswomen of London—a group of fencers who excell. Said Mr. Eddy: 'Chicago women have a great chance to win honors in this sport ... American woman as a rule is too excitable to do a good bout for fencing requires calmness. It should be good practice for the highstrung.' He recommended the sport as a means of keeping young and supple."[14]

[13] Mme X, "Events in Society Circles," *Chicago Daily Tribune*, November 26, 1911, 14.
[14] *Chicago Daily Tribune*, April 5, 1913, 13.

# VIII

## Writings: *Tales of a Small Town, Ganton & Co.*; Plays; and *The New Competition*

While in California, Eddy not only wrote about architecture and fishing, but also turned his attention to fiction. *Tales of a Small Town* by "One Who Lived There" was published somewhat anonymously in 1907.[1] The author dedicated the book to his son, Jerome, on the occasion of his sixteenth birthday. Comprising nine chapters or vignettes, the book evokes life in the fictional town of Budston (not resembling California and probably based on his own youth in Michigan). Two of the stories feature lawyers and judges: "Hugh Doring" tells the story of Joe Giddings and "The Judge's Story" is about John Trufax. Several tales focus on crime and violence. Trufax murders his wife's lover, "Blind Izra" kills a little girl, and "The Village Bully" murders a boy. Another young boy is a pickpocket in "A Jail-Bird." In "Mrs. Dummerford's Niece," Miss Plumm has an affair with her uncle and his best friend. Although Eddy was more adept at expository writing—on most any subject—rather than fiction, he published a novel the following year.

The subject matter of *Ganton & Co.: A Story of Chicago Commercial and Social Life* was familiar to the author even if the romantic subplots were not. John Ganton is the most powerful businessman in the Chicago stockyards, whose office is on LaSalle Street (by coincidence, where Eddy's law firm was located). Ruthless and stubborn, he pays off the unions to avoid a strike, plays his sons against each other in a manipulative manner, and refuses to deal with his illness. The book details corruption in the labor unions as well as drinking at the country clubs. Even before the book came out, it elicited vehement denials by club members. Eddy knew the milieu: He was a member of both the Onwentsia and Saddle and Cycle Clubs in Chicago. Of course he insisted that the book was pure fiction.[2]

*Ganton & Co.* was adapted for the stage as *The Great John Ganton* by J. Hartley Manners.[3] It was presented in Chicago, New York, and Los Angeles in 1909 and widely reviewed. About the same time, Eddy tried his hand at writing plays. In January 1910 the Shuberts decided not to produce his play *The Man Higher Up*. However, *The Warning* was staged at the Hyperion Theater in New Haven and the Shubert Theater in Boston in October 1911. Eddy had two of his

[1] "One Who Lived There," *Tales of a Small Town* (Philadelphia: J. B. Lippincott, 1907). Opposite the title page there is a list of three publications by Arthur Jerome Eddy.

[2] See *Chicago Daily Tribune*, August 30, 1908, 3; August 31, 1908, 10; and November 1, 1908, G3.

[3] Manners's typescript is preserved in the Billy Rose Theatre Division of the New York Public Library for the Performing Arts at Lincoln Center.

plays privately printed: *Scorpio*, a comedy about signs of the zodiac in three acts,[4] and *Hypnotized*, a play in four acts about mining in the West and a French geologist.[5] Yet neither play was produced.

In January 1910 the society columnist for the *Chicago Daily Tribune* reported that: "Arthur J. Eddy is as many sided a man as we may have in Chicago: in fact, he has more sides than most. ... And now he has abandoned old vintages, old and new masters, motor cars, and fish for literature."[6] He had, of course, begun writing decades earlier and never stopped. His efforts in theater and fiction can be dated about 1907 until 1911. By 1911 he was working on *The New Competition: An Examination of the Conditions Underlying the Radical Change that Is Taking Place in the Commercial and Industrial World—The Change from a Competitive to a Coöperative Basis.* Here he is back to facts and what he knows.

As stated in the Foreword:

> This book deals, first of all, with *what is now going on*—with *Facts*; secondly, with the *Principles* underlying actual conditions; thirdly, with *Tendencies* so far as they can be inferred from close and impartial consideration of facts and principles. No attempt has been made to fit facts to a preconceived theory, or stretch any stubbornly held theory to cover unrelated facts ... [The book] is of as much value to the laborer as to the employer, to the country mechanic and merchant as to the large corporation and trust.[7]

He begins with two statements: "competition is the life of trade" and "competition is the death of trade." He proceeds to consider the propositions from different points of view: that of the purchaser, the merchant, the public, the community, and the country.[8] Eddy emphasizes that the old competition is rapidly passing and that the new competition is cooperation. He states that the world has changed; steam and electricity have brought countries and people close together; distance has been well-nigh annihilated. He believes in progress and argues repeatedly for openness and honesty.[9] In

[4] There is a copy in Newberry Library in Chicago.
[5] A copy is located in the New York Public Library.
[6] Mme X, "News of the Society World," *Chicago Daily Tribune*, January 9, 1910, B7.
[7] Arthur Jerome Eddy, *The New Competition: An Examination of the Conditions Underlying the Radical Change that Is Taking Place in the Commercial and Industrial World—The Change from a Competitive to a Coöperative Basis* (New York: D. Appleton and Company, 1912).
[8] Eddy, *The New Competition*, 1.
[9] Eddy, *The New Competition*, see pp. 1–38 and passim.

trying to define competition, he finds it to be synonymous with struggle, contest and rivalry, whereas the foundation of society is cooperation. He faults the antitrust laws as suppressing cooperation and criticizes the Sherman Act of 1890 as being destructive and detrimental to cooperation. He focuses on contemporary legal cases involving American Sugar Refining Company, Standard Oil, General Electric, and on discrepancies between laws in various states as they affect current court cases. His numerous examples range from the steel industry to carpenters' associations to railroad strikes. The book includes specific cases and footnotes as well appendixes dedicated to conditions in Canada, England, and Germany. Throughout, Eddy favors publicity, transparency, and open-price policies over legislation. He sees the need for new legislation that will promote "the frank and free disclosure of competitive practices" and "the suppression of all dishonest, fraudulent, oppressive and unfair business methods."[10]

In 1901 Eddy had published *The Law of Combinations*, in which he considered cooperation to be a positive element in social progress and in communities. By October 1911 his ideas on the new competition and open price associations appeared in *The World's Week.*[11] Eddy's ideas on trade associations would have a strong influence on the thinking of Louis D. Brandeis. Like Eddy, Brandeis advocated regulated competition. He knew Eddy's writings on cooperative competition, his experiments with open price associations, and his belief in sharing information. In 1913 the two men corresponded.[12] Updated editions of *The New Competition* were published by A. C. McClurg & Co. in Chicago in 1913, 1915, 1917, and 1920: thus, the book had a wide audience among lawyers, legislators, students, and the business community.

In writing *The New Competition* Eddy drew on his experience as a lawyer. In March 1911, he and his partner Emil C. Wetten argued the case of Erastus W. Willard against the Chicago, Burlington & Quincy Railway Company before the United States Supreme Court in Washington. Since 1904 Eddy, Haley & Wetten had represented both appellants and appellees in a wide variety of cases. Other cases involving railways were *Chicago & Joliet Electric Railway Company v.*

---

[10] Eddy, *The New Competition*, 339.

[11] *The World's Week* XXII, no. 5 (October 1911): 14954–58.

[12] See Gerald Berk, *Louis D. Brandeis and the Making of Regulated Competition, 1900–1932* (Cambridge, UK: Cambridge University Press, 2009), 63–64, 153–55.

*Samuel Spence* in 1904; *Sanitary District of Chicago v. Pittsburgh, Ft. Wayne & Chicago Railway Company et al.* in 1905; *Illinois, Iowa & Minnesota Railway Company v. Ring* in 1905; *Murphy et al. v. Chicago, Rock Island & Pacific Railway Company* in 1910; and *J. W. Fernald & Co. v. Chicago, Burlington & Quincy Railway Company* in 1912.

# IX

## Art Interests, 1911–12

By 1912 Arthur Eddy already owned a painting by the Dutch modernist Otto Van Rees as well as works by Auguste Herbin and Pablo Picasso. Picasso's *Old Woman* (*Vieille femme*) of 1901 (Figure 9.1) and Herbin's *House and Flowering Cherry Trees, Hamburg* (*Maison et arbres en fleurs, Hambourg*) of 1907 (Figure 9.2) both had labels from Clovis Sagot & Cie. at 46, rue Laffitte in Paris. Clovis Sagot is remembered not only for showing Picasso's work at an early date, but also for having his portrait painted by the artist in 1909.[1] Eddy also owned another Herbin, *Pond and Little House* (*Etang et petite maison*) of 1908, which came from Sagot. These pictures display a heightened palette of bright colors and freely brushed surfaces that contrast with the more subdued work already in his collection. In addition, Eddy owned Herbin's watercolor, *Portrait of His Father* (*Portrait de son père*), which bears a Sagot label; he may have acquired his *Still Life with Vase of Flowers* (*Nature morte au vase de fleurs*) also of 1909 from the same gallery. Moreover, Auguste Chabaud's expressive *Cemetery Gates* (*La porte du cimitière*; Figure 9.3) was purchased from Sagot[2] and work by Van Rees was available at his gallery.[3] Like the Frenchmen Chabaud and Herbin, Picasso and Van Rees belonged to a generation of artists born in the early 1880s who lived primarily in France and exhibited widely in Europe. Eddy illustrated two paintings by Van Rees in his book *Cubists and Post-Impressionism* (1914) and, at the time of his memorial show at the Art Institute (1922), four pictures were included.

We know that Eddy arrived in London on August 1, 1911, tried to visit Rodin in Paris on September 7, and sailed back from Cherbourg on September 23. Most likely, he acquired the above-mentioned pictures from Sagot during this stay as the collector owned them before 1913 and the art dealer died in February of that year. Eddy did not go to Europe between 1903 and 1911; during this interim he spent much of his time in California.

In March 1912 Eddy purchased a remarkably abstract pastel by the American Arthur Dove, *Based on Leaf Forms and Spaces* (Figure 9.4), when the artist had a one-person show at the W. Scott Thurber

[1] John Richardson, *A Life of Picasso: The Prodigy, 1881–1906* (New York: Random House, 1991), 352, 354–355, 389.

[2] Correspondence with Serge Fauchereau, October 24, 2011.

[3] Correspondence with Irène Lesparre, March 7, 2011. Sagot's widow reopened the gallery only in October 1913.

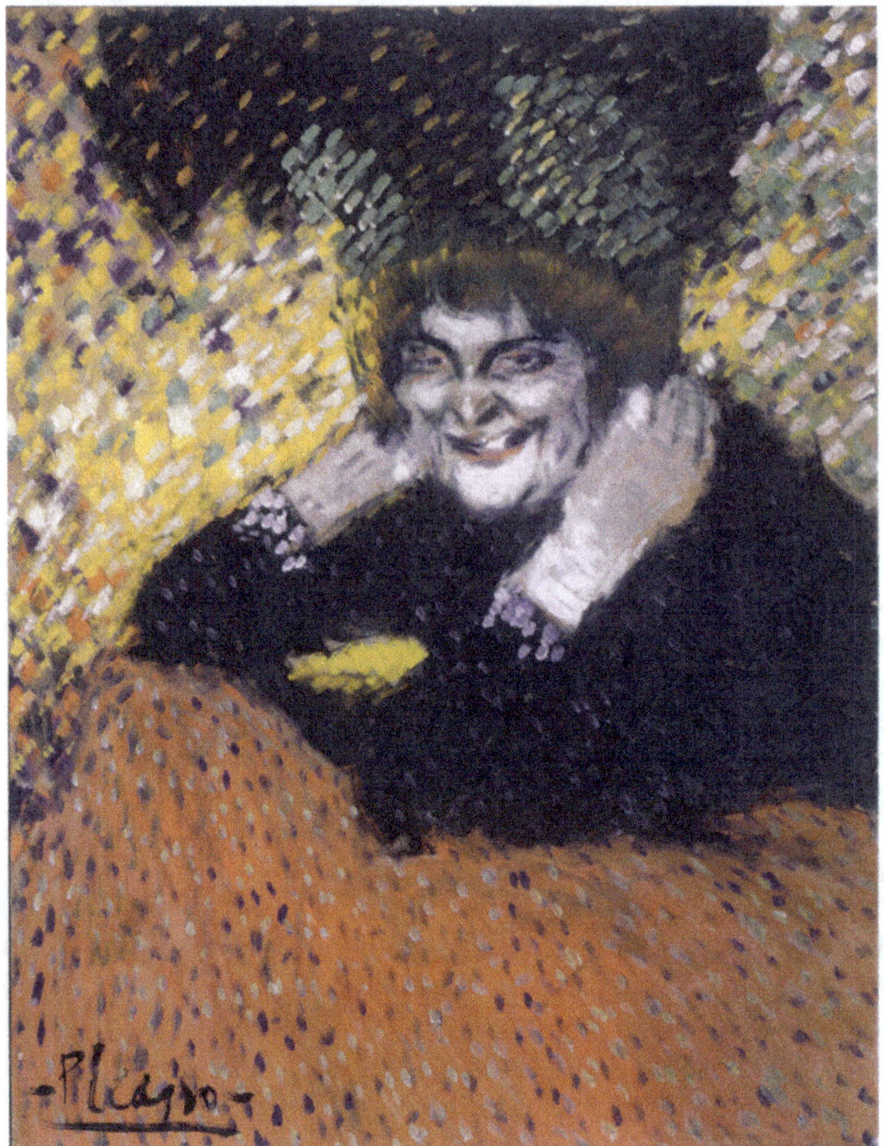


Figure 9.1 Pablo Picasso, *Old Woman* (*Woman with Gloves*), 1901.

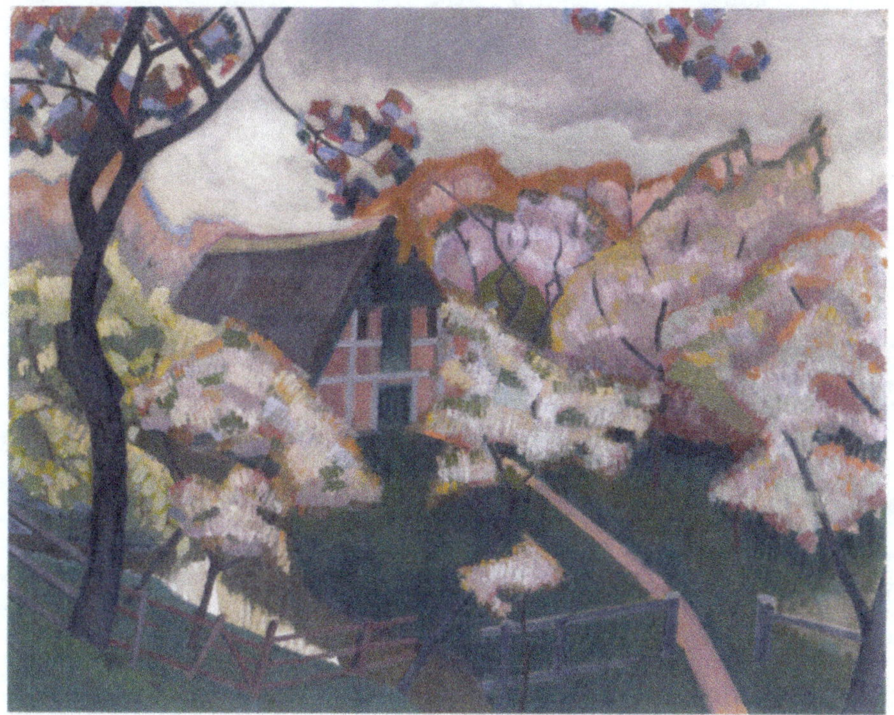

Figure 9.2 Auguste Herbin, *House and Flowering Cherry Trees, Hamburg,* 1907.

The Art Institute of Chicago: Arthur Jerome Eddy Memorial Collection (1931.507)/Art Resource, NY.

Galleries in Chicago.[4] While preparing *Cubists and Post-Impressionism* the following year, Eddy initiated a correspondence with the artist and asked him to "explain as I would talk to any intelligent friend, the idea behind the picture," or "what I am driving at." Dove replied:

> The first step was to choose from nature a motif in color and with that motif to paint from nature, the forms still being objective. The second step was to apply the same principle to form, the actual dependence upon the object (representation) disappearing, and

[4] The exhibition, "Paintings by Arthur Dove," took place March 14 to 30 in Chicago and was presumably the same as what Alfred Stieglitz had shown at the Little Galleries of the Photo-Secession in New York from February 27 to March 12, 1912. See Anne Lee Morgan, *Arthur Dove: Life and Work with a Catalogue Raisonné* (Newark: University of Delaware Press, 1984), 39, 43–44, 104, 320. The pastel is lost and presumably destroyed. It is known from the color reproduction opposite p. 48 in Eddy's book *Cubists and Post-Impressionism* (Chicago: A.C. McClurg & Co., 1914).

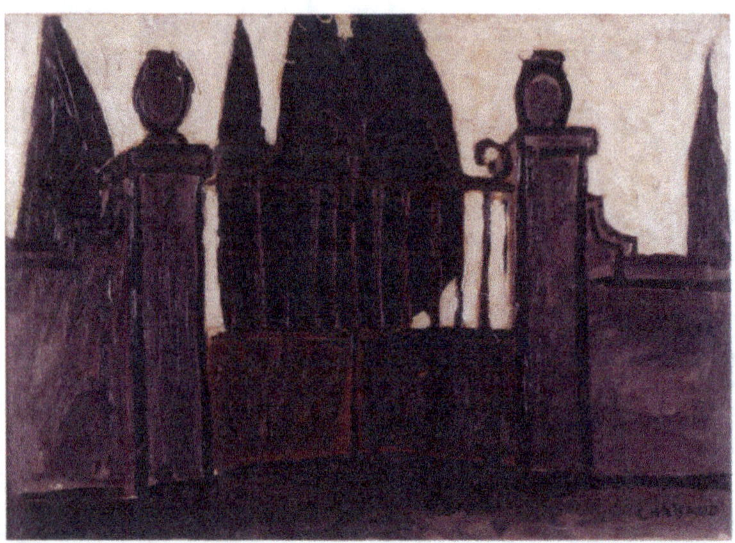

Figure 9.3 Auguste Chabaud, *Cemetery Gates*, c. 1909.
Private collection, Bochum, Germany.

> the means of expression becoming purely objective. After working for sometime in this sway [*sic*], I no longer observed in the old way, and, not only began to think subjectively but also to remember certain sensations purely through their form and color, that is, by certain shapes, planes of light, or character lines determined by the meeting of such planes.[5]

Clearly Eddy's acceptance of modern art predated the Armory Show. Eddy's membership in the Art Institute's Friends of American Art in early 1910 attests to his interest in American as well as European art. Both of his first purchases in the 1890s, as well as his daring acquisitions in 1912–13, accentuate the variety and reveal the evolution of Eddy's taste.

In December 1912 Arthur and his wife, Lucy, went to London for Christmas. Having arrived in Liverpool on the *Carmania* on December 15, they stayed at Queen Anne's Mansions near St. James's

[5] Undated draft of a letter from Dove to Eddy and Eddy's two letters to Dove (from October 12, 1913 and November 6, 1913) are preserved in the Beinecke Rare Book and Manuscript Library, Yale University, New Haven, CT, Alfred Stieglitz/Georgia O'Keeffe Archive, YCAL MSS 85, Box 15, Folder 346.

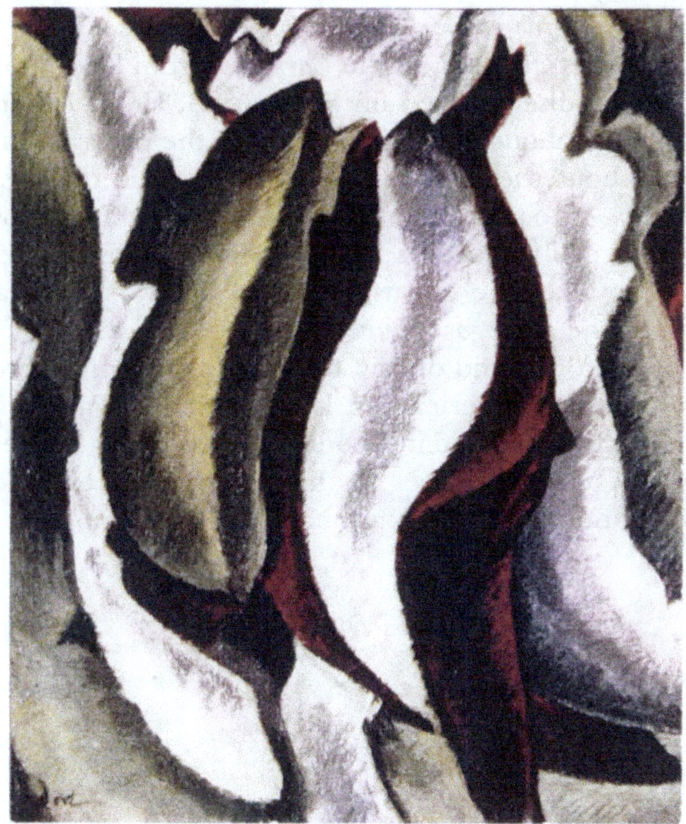

Figure 9.4 Arthur Dove, *Based on Leaf Forms and Spaces*, 1911–12.

Location unknown. Arthur Jerome Eddy, *Cubists and Post-Impressionism* (Chicago, A.C. McClurg & Co., 1914).

Park in London. It is very likely that Eddy went to see the Second Post-Impressionist Exhibition organized by Roger Fry at the Grafton Galleries. There he would have seen works by Chabaud, Herbin, Derain, and Vlaminck as well as many by Picasso and Henri Matisse. In fact, a few of the works he acquired from the Armory Show—for example, the pictures by Derain, Vlaminck, and Eugène Zak—had already been presented in the Second Post-Impressionist Exhibition. Although Eddy had hoped to travel briefly from London to Paris to see Rodin, he wrote to the sculptor on January 21 that he had been too busy to take the trip but that "since I intend to return in May or June, I hope to have the pleasure of seeing you before long." (*Comme j'ai l'intention de revenir au mois de mai ou de juin, j'espère alors avoir le plaisir de vous voir avant bien longtemps.*)[6]

Arthur Eddy returned on the *Carmania* from Liverpool to New York, where he disembarked on February 3. Upon his arrival he would have read about the Armory Show in the press and undoubtedly heard about the dissent among its organizers. The official opening was to take place on February 17 although the show would be open informally two days earlier.[7] Evidently Eddy went back to Chicago to take care of business after his two-month absence. According to the *Chicago Tribune* of February 18, "Arthur J. Eddy, who has been in England during the winter, has come across for a visit of a month to America and is at his Buena Park residence" although his wife remained in London. Signaling his interest in art, Eddy became a Life Member of the Art Institute of Chicago on February 13 and paid $100 in annual dues.

[6] Letter dated January 21, 1913, from Eddy to Rodin, belongs to the Musée Rodin.

[7] See *New York Times*, February 2, 1913, SM14; *New York Times*, February 16, 1916, among other articles; and Harriet Monroe, "Bedlam in Art: A Show that Clamors," *Chicago Daily Tribune*, February 16, 1913, G5.

# X

# The Armory Show, 1913

Following his usual pattern, Arthur Eddy did not remain in Chicago for long, but went back to New York, where he stayed at the Hotel Gotham at Fifth Avenue and 55th Street. Eddy was not alone among Chicagoans traveling to New York to see the Armory Show: Arthur Aldis, Ira Morris, and George Porter also went to New York, where they purchased works out of the show. On February 28, 1913, Mr. Eddy sent a check for $810 to Elmer MacRae, Treasurer of the Association of American Painters and Sculptors, with a covering note written on the hotel letterhead for two paintings he had bought the day before: *The Shepherd* (*Le Berger*, Figure 10.1) by the Polish artist Zak and *The Laborer* (*Le Laboureur*) by the Frenchman Chabaud. These canvases feature a figure seen against a wide, rather unreal landscape. Both artists lived in Paris and lent the works to the Armory Show themselves. A few days later, on Saturday, March 1, Eddy was more daring when he purchased for a total of $1,404, Gleizes's *Man on a Balcony* (*L'Homme au balcon [Portrait de Dr. Théo Morinaud]*; Figure 10.2), Villon's *Young Girl* (*Jeune fille*, Figure 10.3), Duchamp's *Portrait of Chess Players* (*Portrait de joueurs d'échecs*; Figure 10.4), and two landscapes by Segonzac (Figure 10.5). In his selections from the Armory Show, Eddy focused on Cubist and Fauve painters. The following day, Sunday, he boldly bought an even more difficult Duchamp, *The King and Queen Surrounded by Swift Nudes* (*Le Roi et la reine entourné de nus vites*; Figure 10.6), Picabia's radical *Dances at the Spring* (*Danses à la source*, Figure 10.7), Derain's *Forest at Martigues* (*La Forêt à Martigues*; Figure 10.8), Vlaminck's *Rueil* (Figure 10.9), and Kroll's *Terminal Yards* (Figure 10.10). In the paintings by Duchamp, Villon, and Picabia, it is difficult to decipher the figures and to read the compositions. On March 4, Eddy acquired Emilie Charmy's Fauve painting of L'Estaque (Figure 10.11), Edward Manigault's expressive *The Clown* (Figure 10.12), and two decorative panels by William Taylor.[1]

The room with Cubist works, which focused on artists working in Puteaux, attracted the most attention; Duchamp's *Nude Descending a Staircase* (*Nu descendant un escalier*) was singled out for ridicule. This gallery was called the "Chamber of Horrors." Duchamp lent four of his canvases, two of which were purchased by Arthur Eddy

[1] One of Taylor's panels was illustrated in James William Pattison, "Art in an Unknown Tongue," *Fine Arts Journal* XXVIII, no. 5 (May 1913): 206. All the works by European artists were illustrated in Eddy's book *Cubists and Post-Impressionism* but not those by the Americans: Kroll, Manigault, and Taylor.

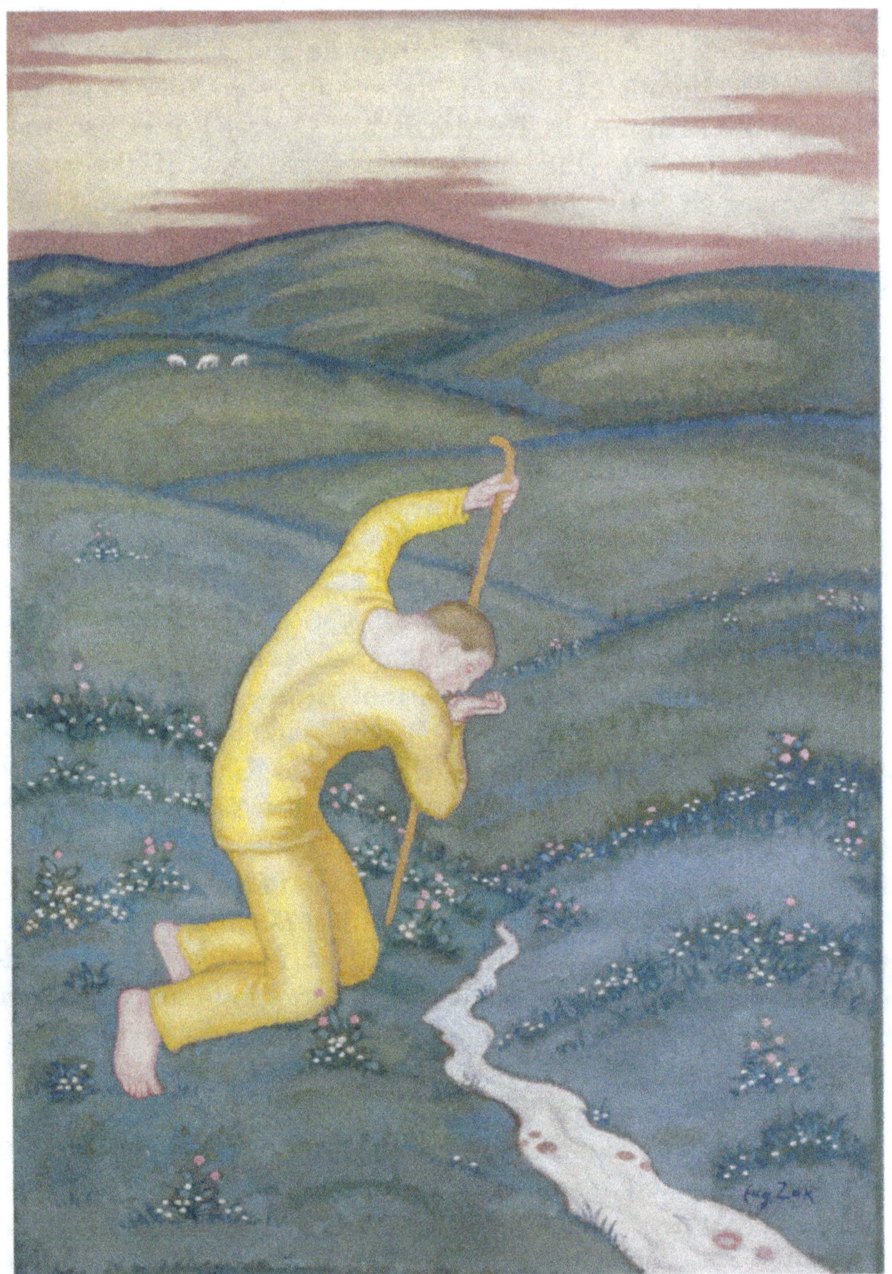

Figure 10.1 Eugène Zak, *The Shepherd*, 1910–11.

The Art Institute of Chicago: Arthur Jerome Eddy Memorial Collection/Art Resource, NY.

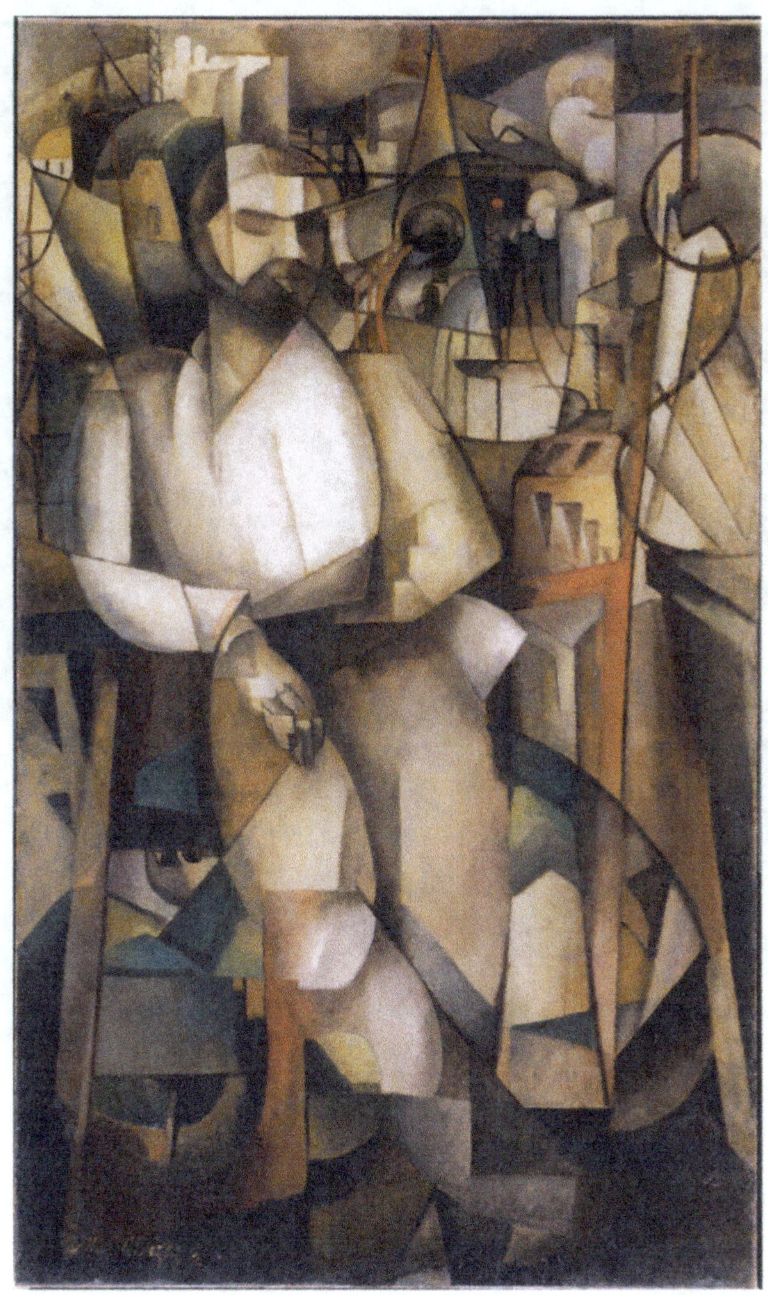

Figure 10.2 Albert Gleizes, *Man on a Balcony* (*Portrait of Dr. Théo Morinaud*), 1912.

Philadelphia Museum of Art: The Louise and Walter Arensberg Collection, 1950 (1950-134-91)/ Art Resource, NY.

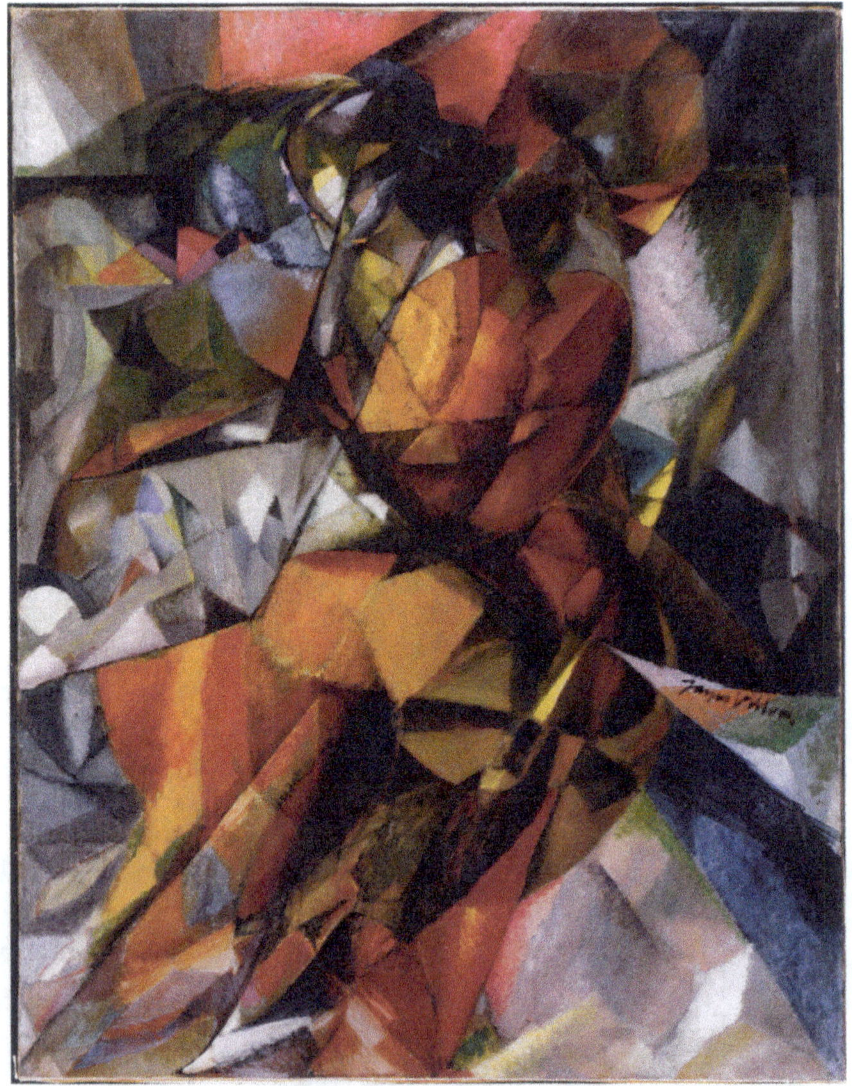

Figure 10.3 Jacques Villon, *Young Girl,* 1912.

Philadelphia Museum of Art: The Louise and Walter Arensberg Collection, 1950 (1950-134-190)/ Art Resource, NY. © 2022 Jacques Villon/ADAGP, Paris.

at the beginning of March. Soon thereafter on March 5, the San Francisco art dealer Frederic C. Torrey bought *Nude Descending a Staircase* and the fourth was later sold to an artist in Chicago. Duchamp's brother Jacques Villon showed nine pictures, one of which was acquired by Eddy, and his other brother, Raymond

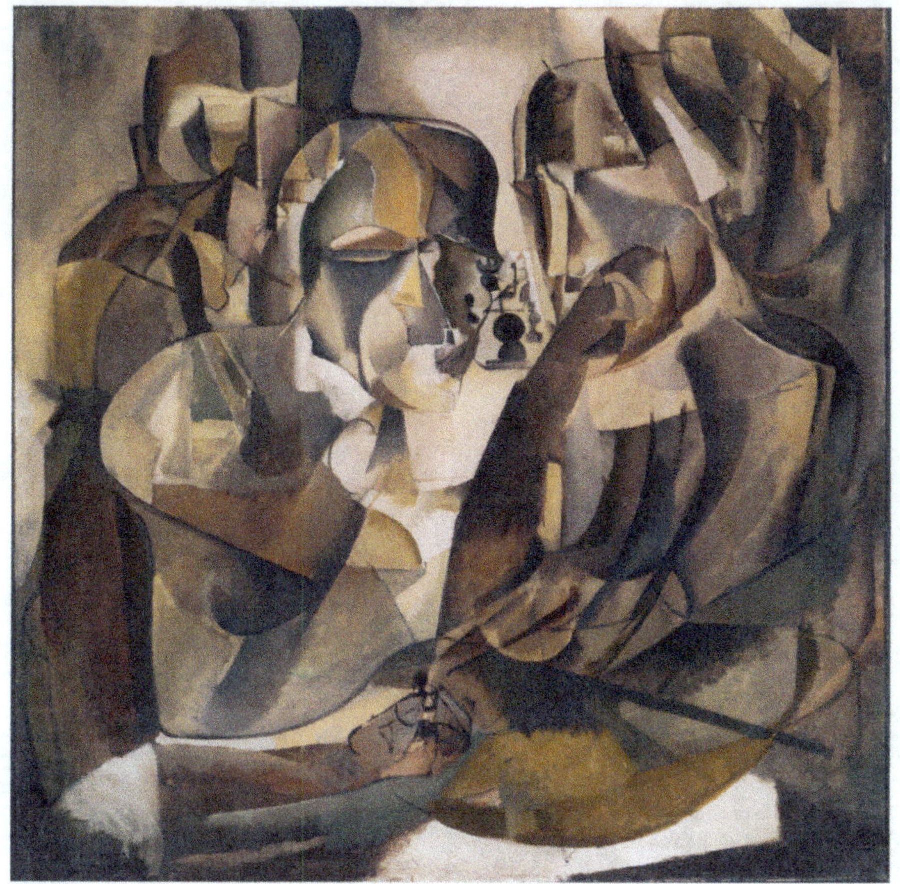

Figure 10.4 Marcel Duchamp, *Portrait of Chess Players,* 1911.

Philadelphia Museum of Art: The Louise and Walter Arensberg Collection, 1950 (1950-134-56)/ Art Resource, NY. © Association Marcel Duchamp/ADAGP, Paris, 2022.

Duchamp-Villon, lent five sculptures. John Quinn selected two of Duchamp-Villon's sculptures and three paintings by Villon, but no works by Duchamp. Eddy, however, did not own any sculptures by Duchamp-Villon. The only European artist who came to New York for the Armory Show was Picabia and Eddy was the only person who acquired his work.

In all, Eddy spent a total of $4,888.50. Only the New York lawyer and collector John Quinn purchased more paintings from the Armory Show and spent more money ($5,808.75) than Arthur

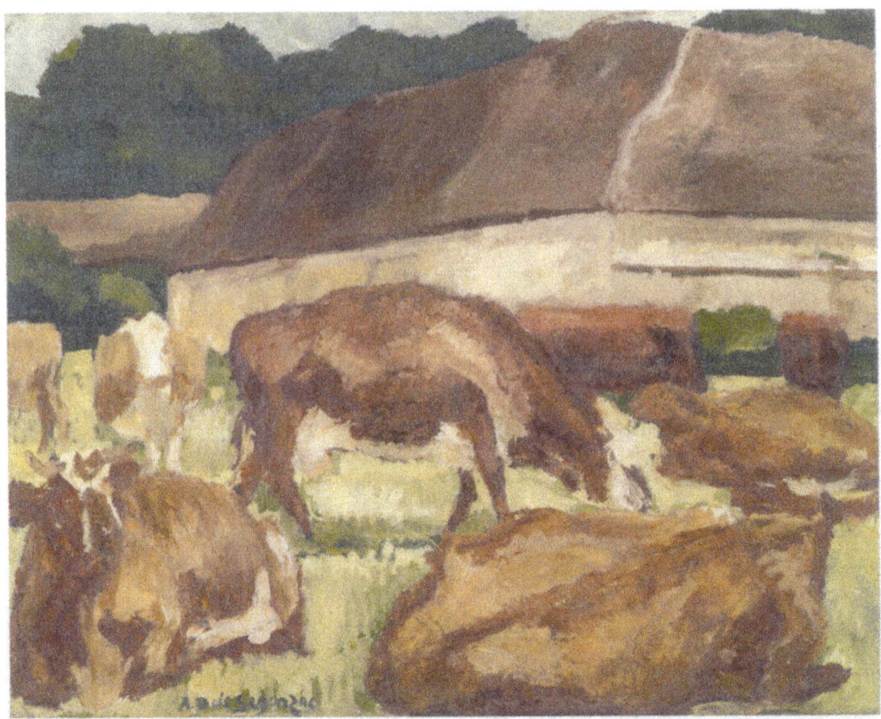

Figure 10.5 André Dunoyer de Segonzac, *Pasturage*, 1912.

The Art Institute of Chicago: Arthur Jerome Eddy Memorial Collection (1931.516)/Art Resource, NY. © 2022 ADAGP, Paris.

Eddy. However, the works he selected were not as radically modern as those purchased by Eddy. Quinn lent many pictures, including a painting by Chabaud, to the show and he bought works by Derain, Segonzac, Villon, and Zak—as did Eddy. In addition, Quinn served as legal counsel to the Association and, thus, was involved with the exhibition.

Walt Kuhn, Secretary of the Association of American Painters and Sculptors, later recalled that John Quinn's "purchase of between five and six thousand dollars worth of pictures reached the ears of Arthur Jerome Eddy,"[2] thus, implying that Eddy was following Quinn. The fact that Kuhn advised Quinn (and had persuaded him to buy) may have colored his perception of who was more influential. He did allow that "Eddy bought some of the most radical works in

[2] Walt Kuhn, *Story of the Armory Show* (New York: Privately printed, 1938), 19.

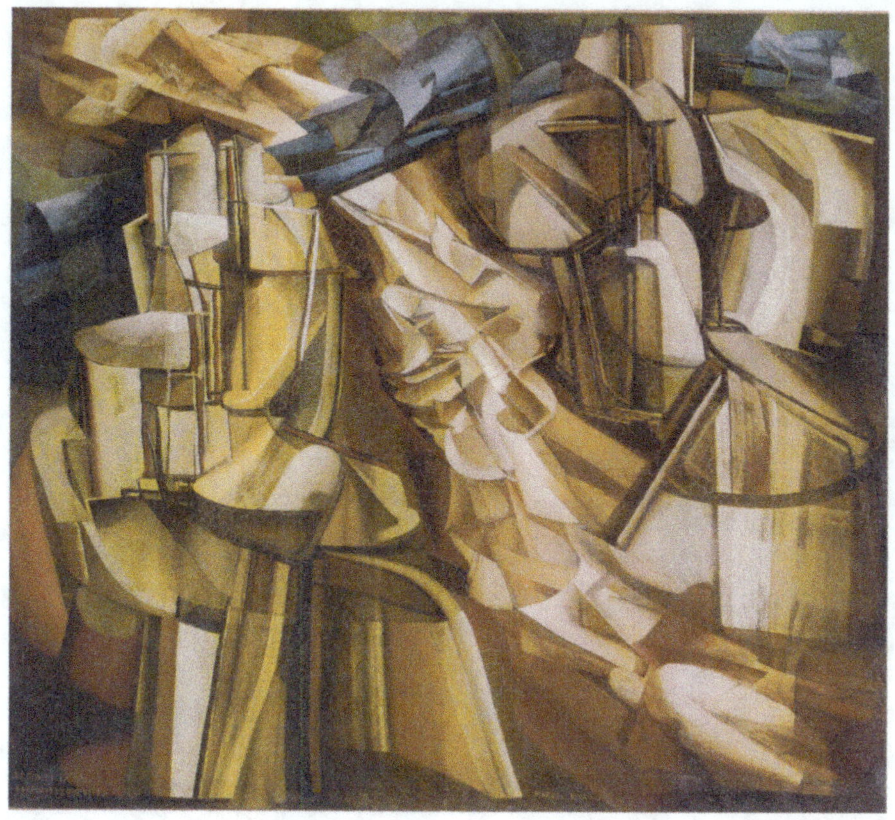

Figure 10.6 Marcel Duchamp, *The King and Queen Surrounded by Swift Nudes*, 1912.

Philadelphia Museum of Art: The Louise and Walter Arensberg Collection, 1950 (1950-134-63a)/ Art Resource, NY. © Association Marcel Duchamp/ADAGP, Paris, 2022.

our show." In any case, Eddy acquired three paintings that had been exhibited in London in late 1912 when he was there: Derain's *Forest at Martigues*, Vlaminck's *Rueil*, and Zak's *The Shepherd*. Certainly Eddy was well informed about the Second Post-Impressionist Exhibition as well as the Armory Show. He prided himself on being the first to know what was new.

On March 15, 1913, Eddy wrote to Arthur B. Davies, President of the Association of American Painters and Sculptors:

> I have told Mr. French of the Art Institute that all the pictures I purchased would come on to Chicago, and that includes the paint-

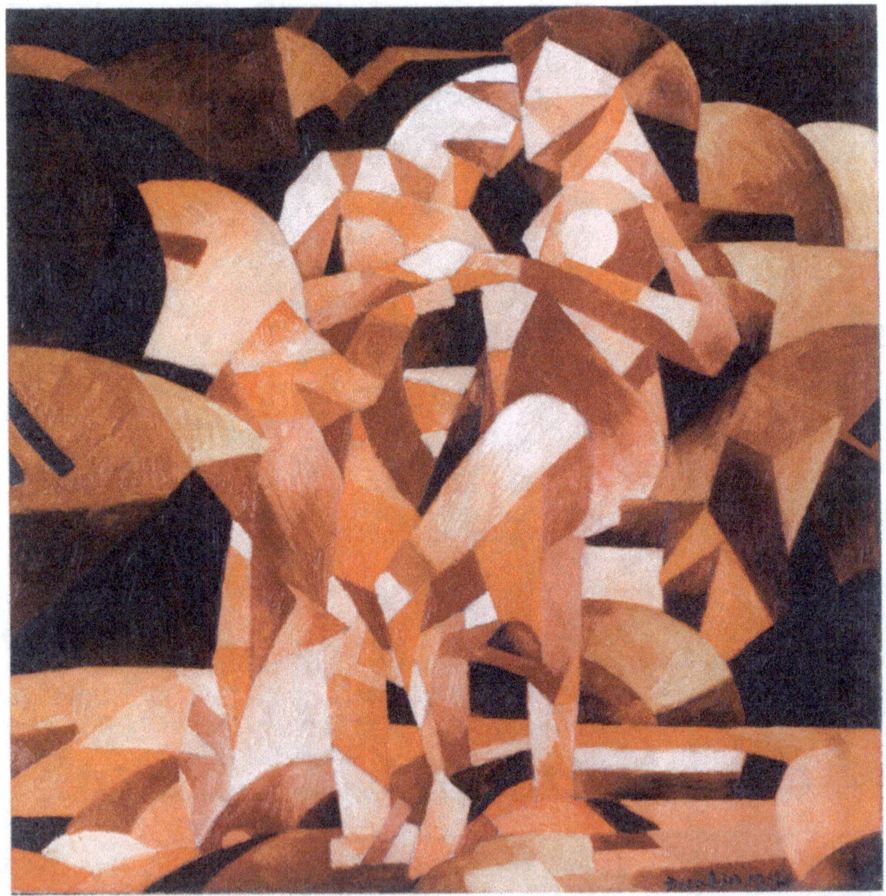

Figure 10.7 Francis Picabia, *Dances at the Spring,* 1912.

Philadelphia Museum of Art: The Louise and Walter Arensberg Collection, 1950 (1950-134-155)/ Art Resource, NY. © 2022 ADAGP, Paris.

> ing by Kroll; two by Taylor and one by Manigault, all Americans. I particularly desire that these pictures be exhibited with the foreign pictures I purchased, because taken all together they illustrate my attitude in art, which is exceedingly catholic. While if the foreign pictures alone were exhibited, it would naturally give rise to the inference that I had lost interest in the strong and virile American pictures.[3]

[3] Letter dated March 15, 1913, from Eddy to Davies, is preserved with the Walt Kuhn Papers, Archives of American Art, Smithsonian Institution, Washington, DC, Box 1, Folder 10.

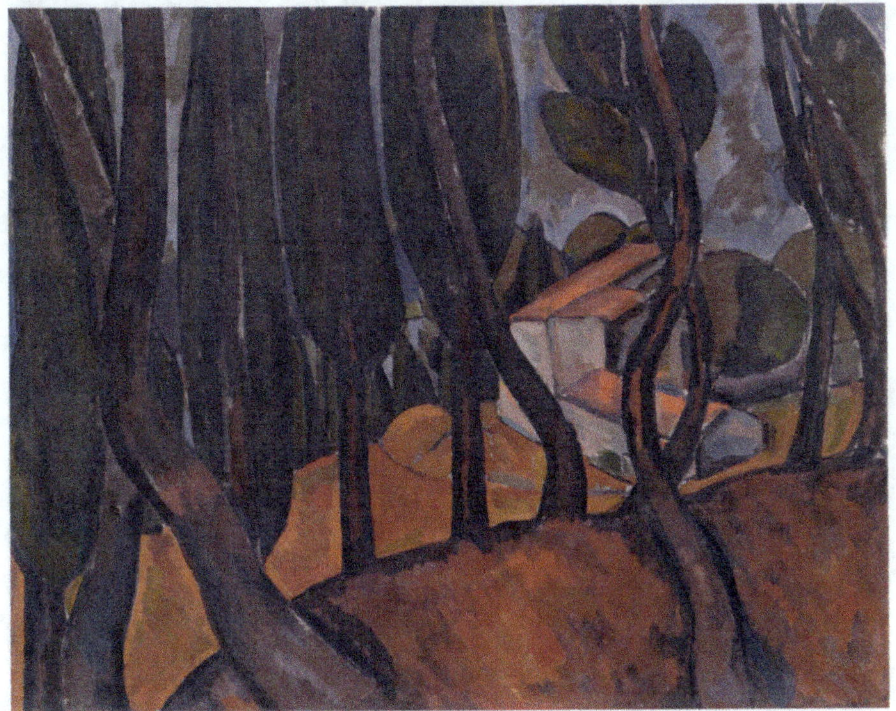

Figure 10.8 André Derain, *Forest at Martigues*, c. 1908/09.

The Art Institute of Chicago: Arthur Jerome Eddy Memorial Collection (1931.506)/Art Resource, NY.

Although it has been suggested that Eddy was having "second thoughts" about the European avant-garde,[4] he may have simply wanted to emphasize how many pictures he had purchased.

With pressure from different factions pro and con and considerable trepidation, Arthur Aldis had arranged for the Armory Show to travel to the Art Institute of Chicago. After the show had opened on March 24, Kuhn wrote from Chicago to Davies:

> Since I started to write this note, Mr. Eddy has changed his tune. He gave a lecture Friday to about a thousand people in Fullerton hall, endorsing the Association and asking fair play for the exhibitors. This is the direct result of our asserting our rights to him at last Sunday's seance. This Chicago business looked a bit difficult at first, but we have the situation well in hand.[5]

[4] Milton W. Brown, *The Story of the Armory Show* (New York: Abbeville Press, 1988), 194.
[5] Letter dated March 29 from Kuhn to Davies is quoted in Brown, 1988, 208.

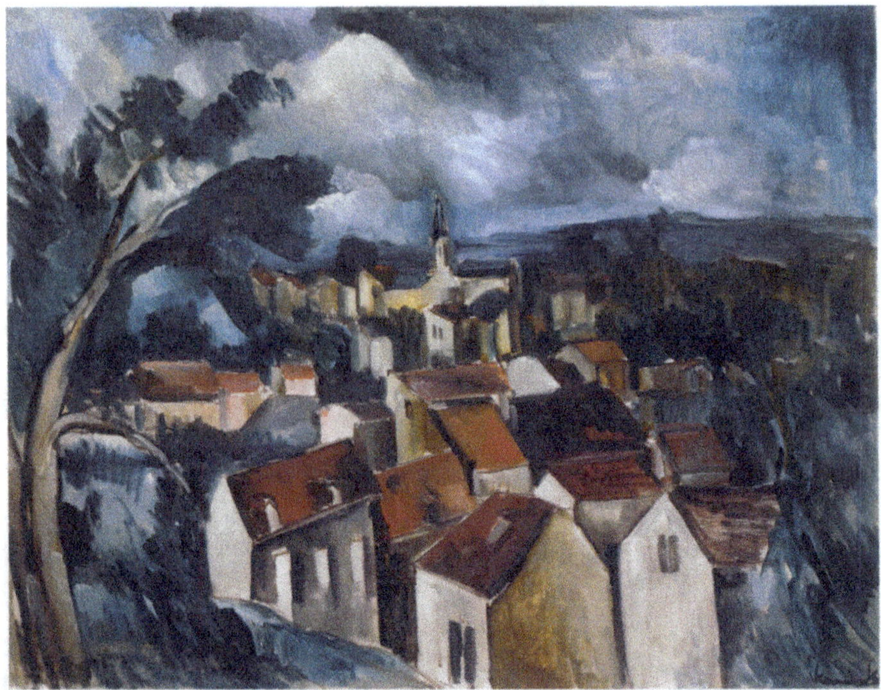

Figure 10.9 Maurice de Vlaminck, *Village (Rueil)*, c. 1912.

The Art Institute of Chicago: Arthur Jerome Eddy Memorial Collection (1931.517)/ Art Resource, NY.

Perhaps the organizers worried that Eddy would criticize the Association. We do not know what was actually said at the meeting on Sunday, the day before the show opened. However, from the *Chicago Daily Tribune,* we know that the same Sunday evening, the Ira Morrises gave a dinner for forty at the Cliff Dwellers Club that was attended by the Eddys, the Arthur Aldises, and Harriet Monroe: "Arthur J. Eddy made a very clever speech linking the cubists, post-impressionists, and futurists with the political upheaval in this country (he called Roosevelt a typical futurist); he further allied them with everything modern, our fashions, our point of view, women's suffrage."[6]

[6] Mme X, "News of the Society World," in *Chicago Daily News,* March 30, 1913, H3. There were actually no Futurists included in the Armory Show.

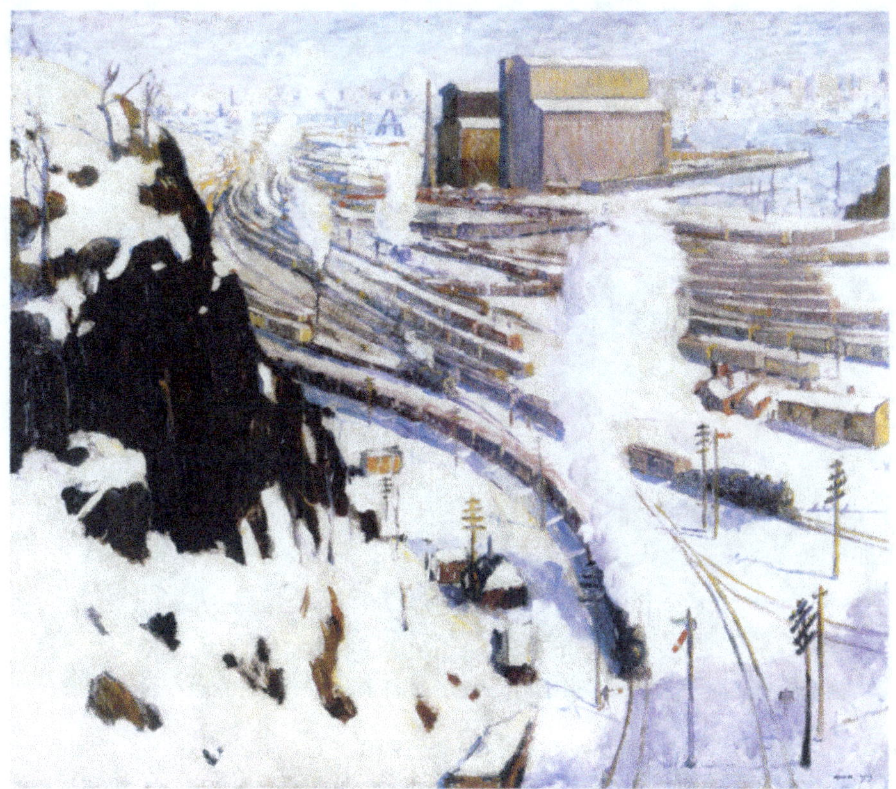

Figure 10.10 Leon Kroll, *Terminal Yards*, 1913.

Flint Institute of Arts, Flint, Michigan: Gift of Mrs. Arthur Jerome Eddy (1931.4).

On the day before the Armory Show opened in Chicago, an article appeared in the same newspaper titled "Here She Is: White Outline Shows 'Nude Descending a Staircase'" announcing that "Arthur J. Eddy, Chicago art dilettante and patron of the new school, has discovered the woman's figure amongst the chaotic jumble of wedges which impress laymen as a representation of an explosion in a shingle factory. ... On Thursday at the Art Institute ... Mr. Eddy will demonstrate his diagram in his lecture on the new schools of art."[7] The article reproduced his diagram (Figure 10.13) and gave instructions on how to see the figure—all advance publicity not only

[7] "Here She Is: White Outline Shows 'Nude Descending a Staircase'," *Chicago Daily Tribune*, March 24, 1913, 5. See Francis M. Naumann, *The Recurrent, Haunting Ghost: Essays on the Art, Life and Legacy of Marcel Duchamp* (New York: Readymade Press, 2012), 25–26.

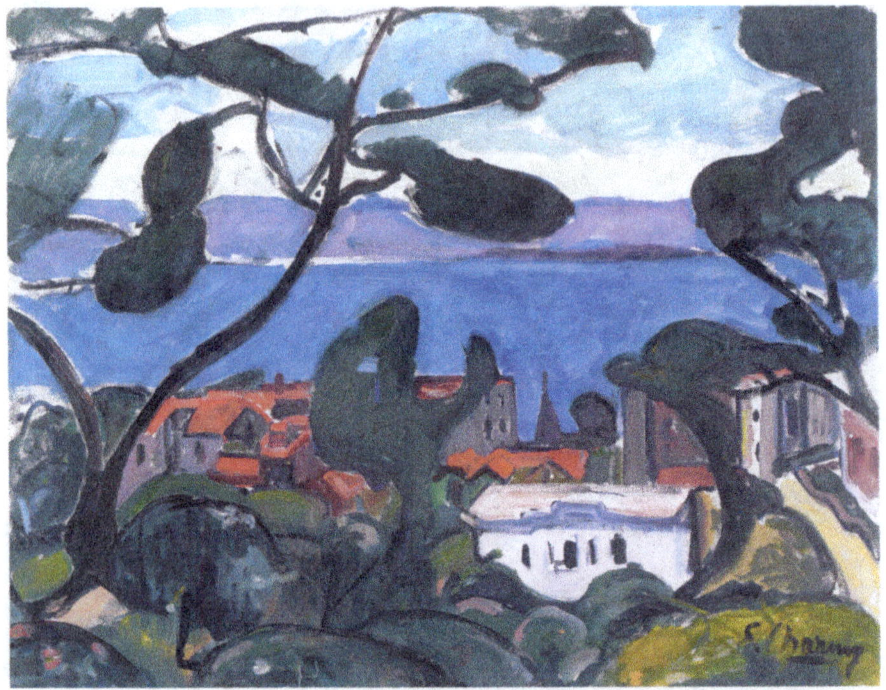

Figure 10.11 Emilie Charmy, *L'Estaque*, c. 1910.

The Art Institute of Chicago/Art Resource, NY: Arthur Jerome Eddy Memorial Collection.

for the show but also for Arthur Eddy's talk. His slide lecture on Cubism on Thursday, March 27 was a great success and he gave another talk on April 3 for all the people who could not be accommodated in Fullerton Hall the week before. According to a newspaper article, Eddy elaborated on why he considered President Woodrow Wilson to be a Cubist, Secretary of State William Jennings Bryan to be an Impressionist, and former President Theodore Roosevelt a "happy Futurist" who admired the new art although Eddy didn't quote from Roosevelt's scathing review of the Armory Show. Instead Eddy referred to the paintings as "beautiful color conceptions and ... congratulated himself on having bought several of them."[8]

When the Armory Show was in Chicago, on April 10 Eddy purchased three paintings by the Portuguese artist Souza Cardoso,

[8] "President Wilson a Cubist? Sure! Art Collector Says," *Chicago Daily Tribune*, April 4, 1913, 9.

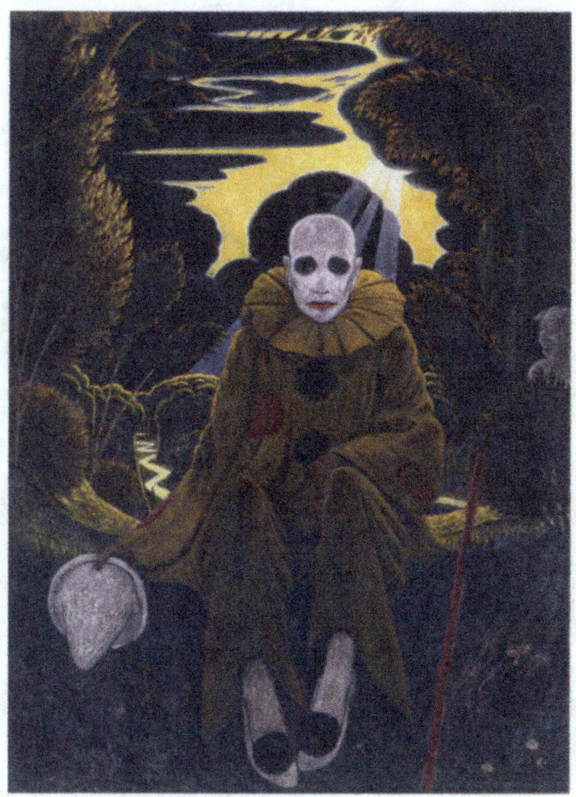

Figure 10.12 Edward Manigault, *The Clown*, 1912.

Columbus Museum of Art, Ohio: Museum: Purchase, Howald Fund.

*The Leap of the Rabbit* (*Saut de lapin*; Figure 10.14), *The Stronghold* (*Château fort*; Figure 10.15), and *Landscape* (*Paysage*) as well as several prints by Maurice Denis and Edouard Vuillard. Souza Cardoso, who lived in Paris and knew many of the Cubists, exhibited eight pictures in the Armory Show. In discussing Eddy's purchase of the Souza Cardosos, Milton Brown wrote that, "these latter, unimportant and only superficially modernist, are an anti-climax to the daring of his earlier selections and seem almost the expression of uncertainty. Perhaps he was momentarily overwhelmed by his own rashness and had his moments of doubt. ... His vacillation was short-lived and he was soon back in the race not only buying the latest manifestations of contemporary art but fighting for its recognition."[9] However, in

[9] Brown, *Armory Show*, 124.

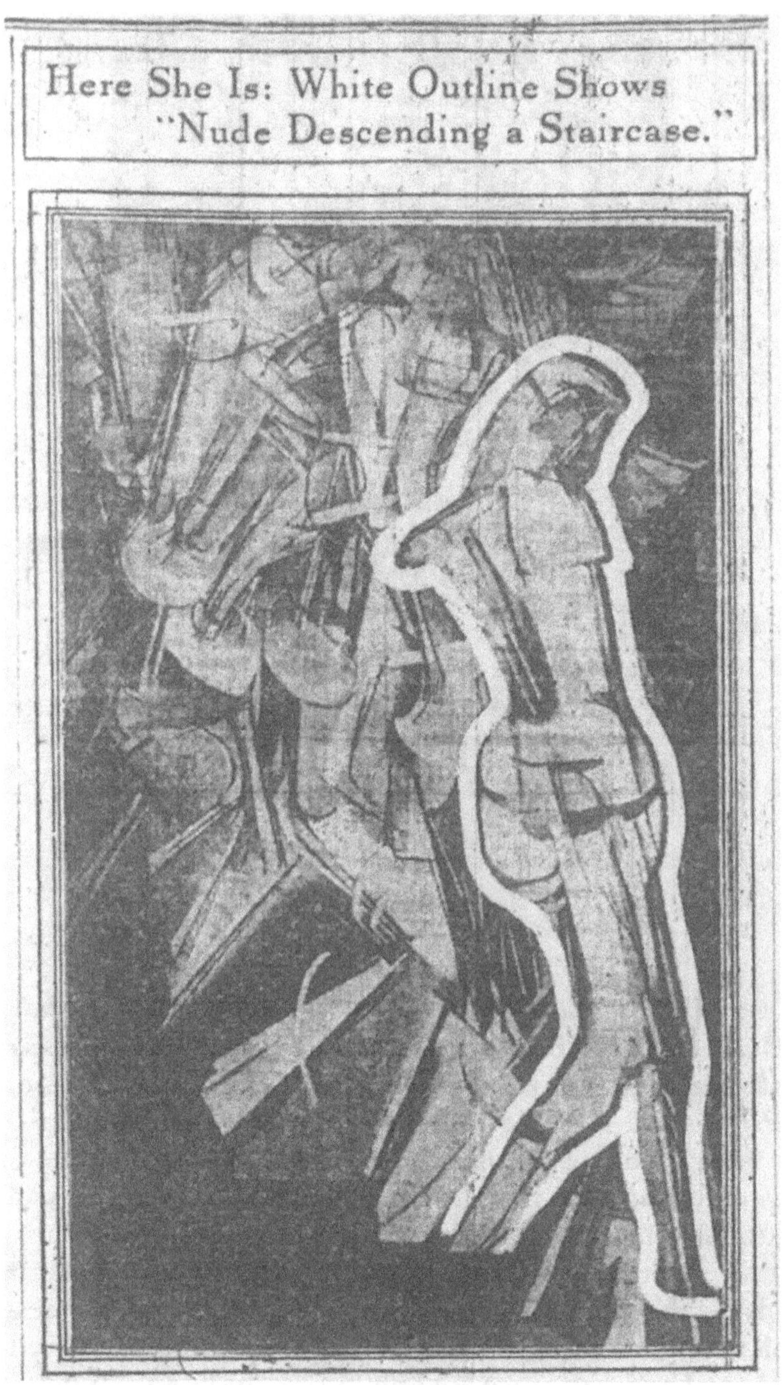


Figure 10.13 A. J. Eddy's diagram of *Nude Descending the Staircase.*

*Chicago Daily Tribune* (March 24, 1913), 5.

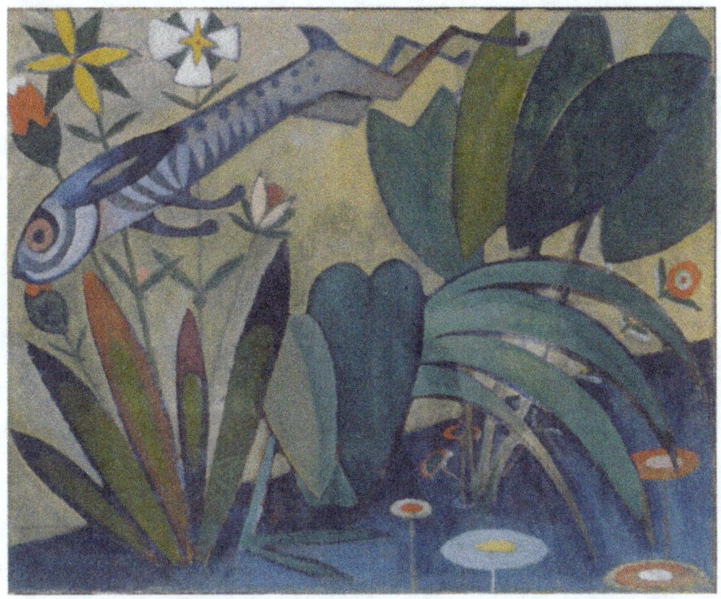

Figure 10.14 Amadeo de Souza Cardoso, *The Leap of the Rabbit,* 1911.

The Art Institute of Chicago: Arthur Jerome Eddy Memorial Collection (1931.514)/Art Resource, NY.

considering Eddy's previous pattern of collecting, there was always great variety in what he chose. Around 1894 he bought Monet's *Snow Effect at Falaise* and Homer's *Coast of Maine*: two vastly different landscapes that might be seen as contradictory tendencies. Likewise, Chabaud's *Cemetery Gates* and Dove's *Based on Leaf Forms and Spaces* seem to have nothing in common. Duchamp's *The King and Queen Surrounded by Swift Nudes* and Zak's *The Shepherd* appear to be completely different. So do Picabia's *Dances at the Source* and Souza Cardoso's *The Leap of the Rabbit.* What unites them all is the collector's remarkably eclectic taste, open to various styles, points of view, and nationalities. Simply said, he bought what he liked.

Not only Arthur Eddy but also Manierre Dawson, a twenty-five-year-old Chicago artist who worked as an architectural draughtsman for Holabird and Roche, bought works by Souza Cardoso and Duchamp. In early April he purchased Souza Cardoso's *Return from the Chase* (*Retour de la chasse*) and Duchamp's *Sad Young Man on a Train* (*Jeune homme triste dans un train*). His own paintings were

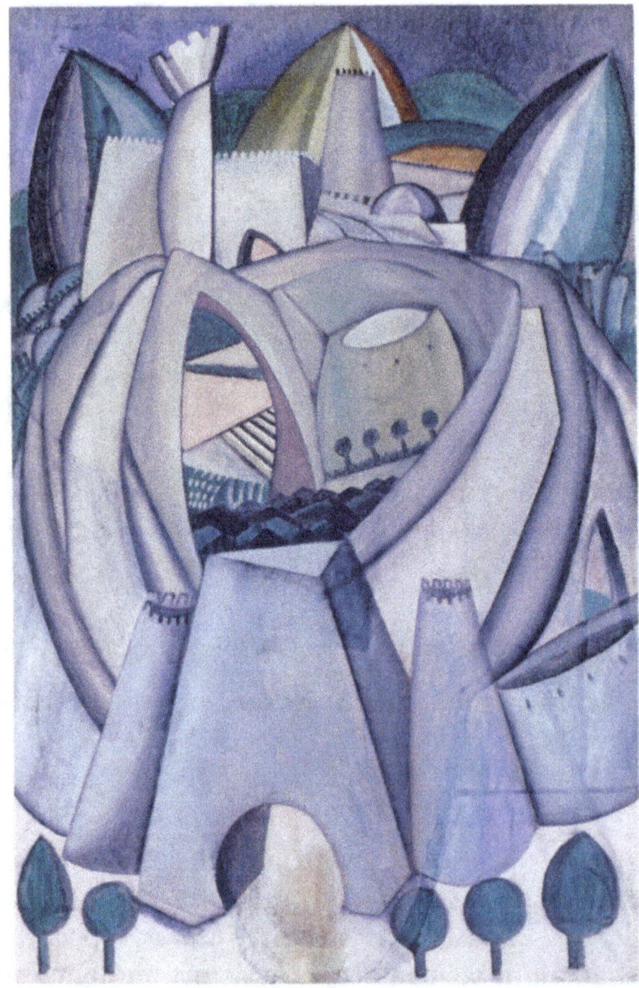

Figure 10.15 Amadeo de Souza Cardoso, *The Stronghold*, 1912.

The Art Institute of Chicago: Arthur Jerome Eddy Memorial Collection (1931.512)/Art Resource, NY.

remarkably abstract well before he saw the Armory Show. Dawson wrote about the exhibition in his journal: "I go to the Art. Inst. every day. This is the most important exhibition ever presented in Chicago. It is having terrific impact on the public. The turnstile count has never been so great. The whole show is producing in me a great excitement ... These are without question the most exciting days of my life. The works of Matisse and Kandinsky are extremely important in breaking open the avenues of freedom of expression. I am feeling elated. I had thought of myself as an anomaly and had to defend myself, many times, as not crazy; and here now at the Art Institute many artists are presented showing these very inventive departures from the academies."[10]

[10] Manierre Dawson Journal, March 27, 1913, Manierre Dawson Papers, Archives of American Art. Transcribed in Randy J. Ploog, Myra Bairstow, and Ani Boyajian, eds., *Manierre Dawson (1887–1969) A Catalogue Raisonné* (New York: The Three Graces, in association with Hollis Taggart Galleries, 2011), 323.

# XI

## Trip to London and Munich: Kandinsky, Jawlensky, and Genin, 1913

As planned, Eddy went to Europe for the summer of 1913, sailing from New York on the *Minnehaha* on May 24, and arriving in London on June 3. In July he purchased all three of Vasily Kandinsky's paintings and Constantin Brancusi's bronze head of the *Sleeping Muse* (*La Muse endormie*; Figure 11.1) from the sixth annual London Salon of the Allied Artists' Association at Royal Albert Hall in London. At the Armory Show Eddy would have seen a plaster of the *Sleeping Muse* as well as Kandinsky's *Improvisation 27* lent by Hans Goltz's Munich gallery and purchased by Alfred Stieglitz. *Improvisation No. 29* (Figure 11.2) and *Improvisation No. 30* (Figure 11.3) belonged to the same series of large abstract works. Eddy was already familiar with these artists' very modern work and seized the opportunity to add Kandinsky's two *Improvisations*, his *Landscape with Two Poplars* (*Landschaft mit zwei Pappeln*), and Brancusi's bronze head to his collection. Moreover, later that month, he traveled to Munich where he went to galleries and artists' studios. German and Russian art had not been well represented in the Armory Show, which favored the Cubists and other French artists.

Arthur Eddy purchased works by three Russian artists living in Munich: two paintings by Robert Genin, probably nine by Alexei Jawlensky, and at least a dozen pictures by Kandinsky. Although it is often stated that the collector and the artist met in Munich or Murnau, Eddy did not meet Kandinsky for the simple reason that the artist was in Russia for the summer (his companion, Gabriele Münter, was in Bonn). Upon his return to London, Eddy wrote to Kandinsky, who was in Moscow, and enclosed the agreed-upon sum of 1,000 German marks:

> The amounts I gave for your pictures were not large but I have bought more pictures than I can afford, far more than I had any intention of buying. I have bough[t] them because I have a philosophic interest in the modern movement and I need enough pictures to demonstrate my theories as well as for my own personal enjoyment. ... I was very sorry you were not in Munich but your very intelligent servant said she was authorized the [*sic*] show me your things and I spent an interesting and valuable two hours looking at your paintings and sketches.[1]

Writing from Chicago on September 23, he told Kandinsky that he had purchased his work and also that of Genin and Jawlensky while in Munich:

[1] Letter in English dated August 18, 1913, from Eddy to Kandinsky, Wassily Kandinsky Papers, Special Collections, The Getty Research Institute, Los Angeles.

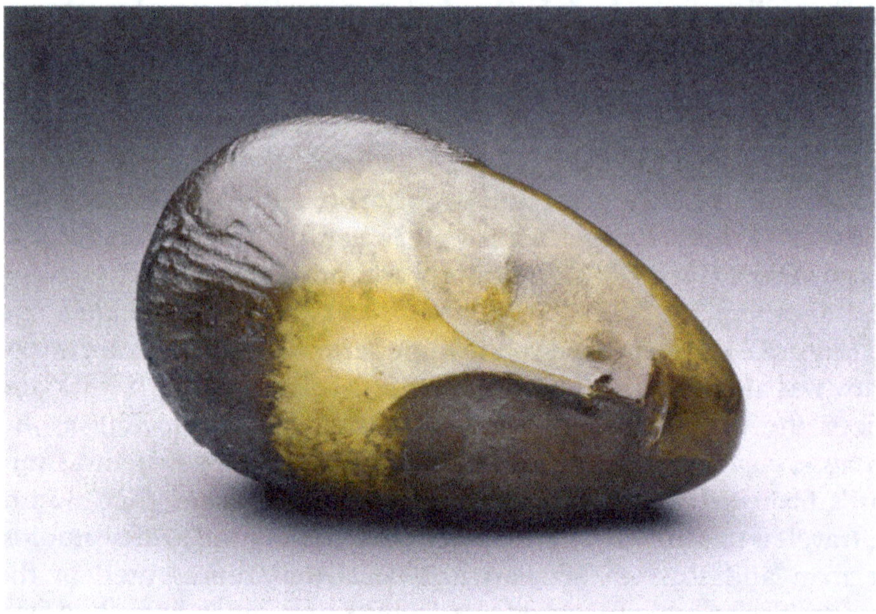

Figure 11.1 Constantin Brancusi, *Sleeping Muse*, 1910.

The Art Institute of Chicago: Arthur Jerome Eddy Memorial Collection (1931.523)/Art Resource, NY. 

> I purchased more of yours, because a very brief glance at your work in your studio showed that you were a master draftsman, and you know it is commonly charged by critics and others, that the new men paint as they do because they cannot draw, and because they cannot paint in the older methods. I thought it worth while to bring back a range of your pictures showing your skill as a draftsman, and your ability to paint in the older methods. Buying as I do I am obliged to buy them at a very reasonable price, that is why frequently I do not feel warranted in making any higher offer for a picture than I do. The pictures I buy would not find ready sale in this country, even if I wished to sell them, and so far I have never sold a picture.[2]

[2] Letter in English dated September 23, 1913, from Eddy to Kandinsky, Wassily Kandinsky Papers, Special Collections, The Getty Research Institute, Los Angeles.

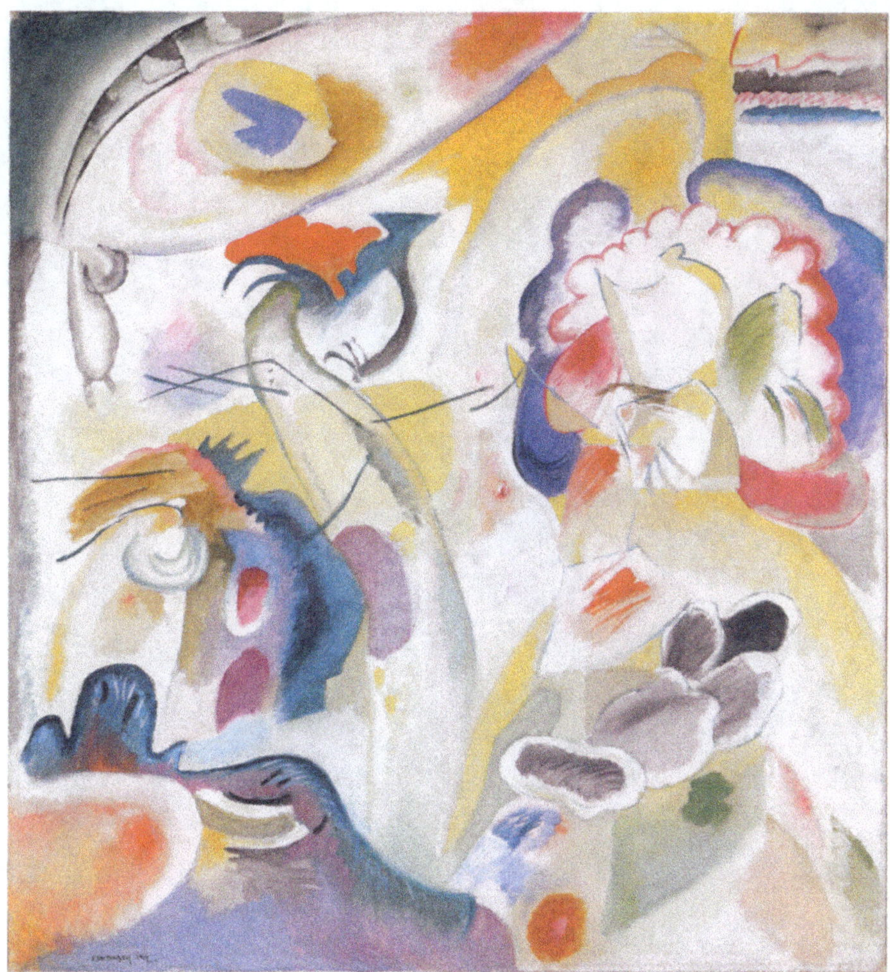

Figure 11.2 Vasily Kandinsky, *Improvisation No. 29* (*The Swan*), 1912.

Philadelphia Museum of Art: The Louise and Walter Arensberg Collection, 1950 (1950-134-102)/ Art Resource, NY.

Eddy selected paintings ranging in date from 1901 to 1911 to complement the three Kandinskys he had purchased in London. These included atypical early works, such as *Trysting Place I* (*Stelldichein I*) of 1901, *Crusaders* (*Kreuzfahrer*) of 1903, and *Sheep Festival* (*Fête de moutons*) of 1905 (Figure 11.4), as well as landscapes painted in Dresden, Paris, Munich, and Murnau. He favored the colorful and freely painted landscapes, *Murnau: View with Castle, Church and Railway* (*Murnau: Ansicht mit Burg, Kirche und Eisenbahn*) and *Murnau:*

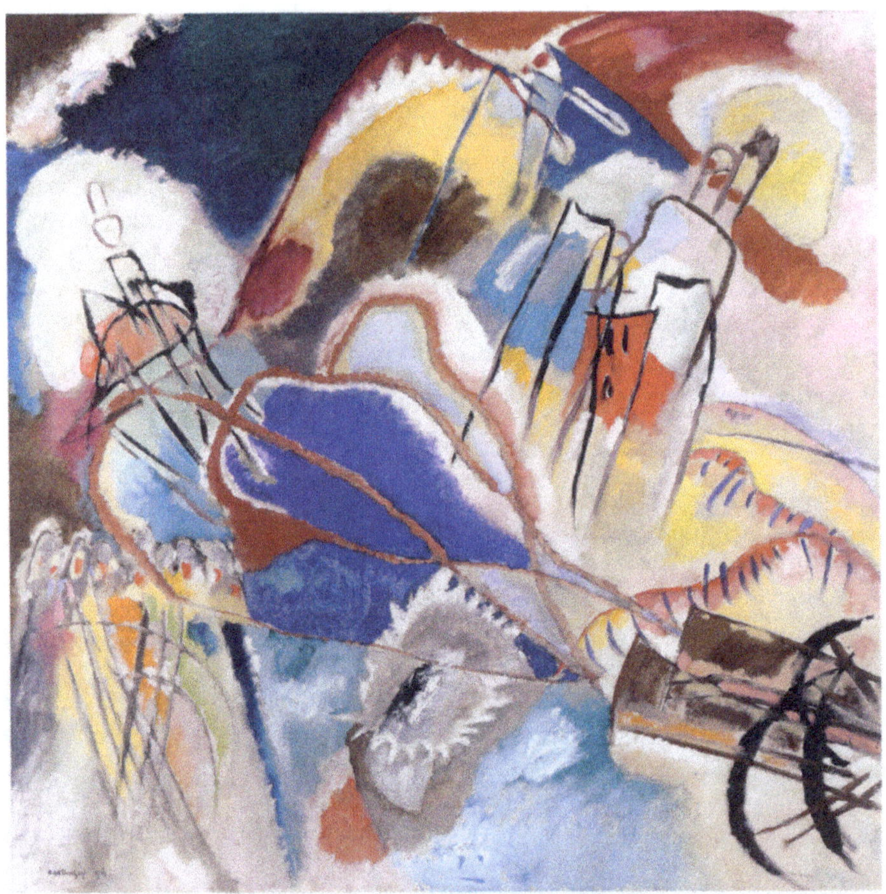

Figure 11.3 Vasily Kandinsky, *Improvisation No. 30* (*Cannons*), 1913.
The Art Institute of Chicago: Arthur Jerome Eddy Memorial Collection (1931.511).

*Landscape with Church I* (*Murnau: Landschaft mit Kirche I*) of 1909 (Figure 11.5), which preceded the more abstract Improvisations. The colorful Tunisian sheep festival painted in tempera on dark cardboard and the large Murnau *Landscape with Church I* both reveal a fluidity of drawing with paint, although one does not immediately think of drawing per se. Eddy also chose the unusual *Painting with Troika* (*Bild mit Troika*) of 1911 (Figure 11.6) with its rare hand-painted frame done in the style of Bavarian folk art. Here the expressive line and puzzling subject matter evoke another world, a non-naturalistic realm.

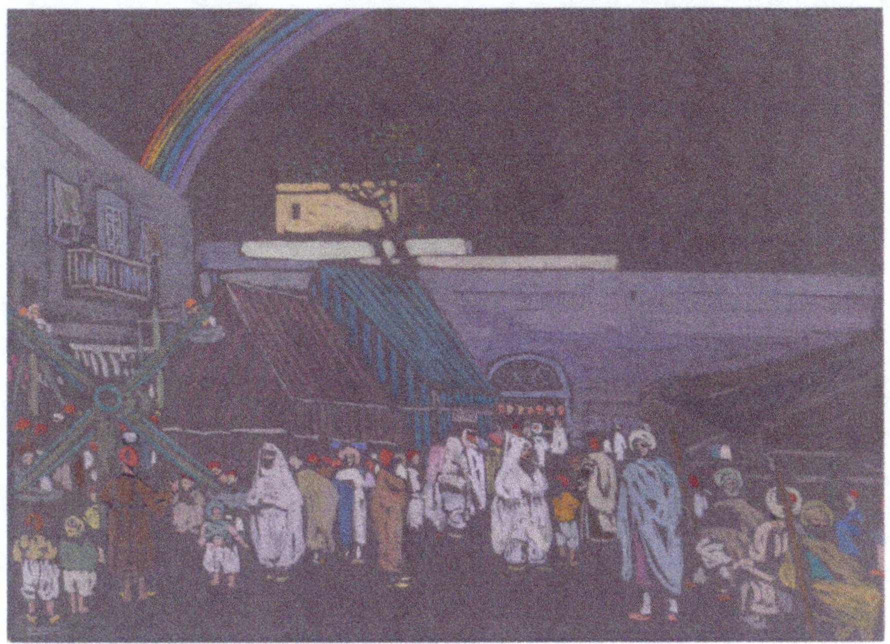

Figure 11.4 Vasily Kandinsky, *Sheep Festival*, 1905.
Solomon R. Guggenheim Museum.

In his book *Cubists and Post-Impressionism*, which appeared in 1914, Eddy wrote: "I have before me six of Jawlensky's heads, painted a year or so apart. They range from almost conventional portrait studies in strong impressionistic manner to heads very like Matisse's 'Madras Rouge,' thence to the head reproduced, which was the last painted [Figure 11.7]. The series shows an interesting development of the painter's *convictions*, his technic remains essentially the same, facile and competent, only the latest picture places a much greater stress upon his resources." Eddy went on to relate: "When asked why he preferred his latest work to the earlier, Jawlensky said 'I have put more of myself into them; they are more expressive of what I feel.'"[3] Evidently Eddy met Jawlensky although it is not known who accompanied him and facilitated communication. The contact was probably made through either Heinrich Thannhauser's Moderne Galerie, where he acquired works by Genin, or Hans Goltz's

[3] Arthur Jerome Eddy, *Cubists and Post-Impressionism* (Chicago: A. C. McClurg & Co., 1914), 113.

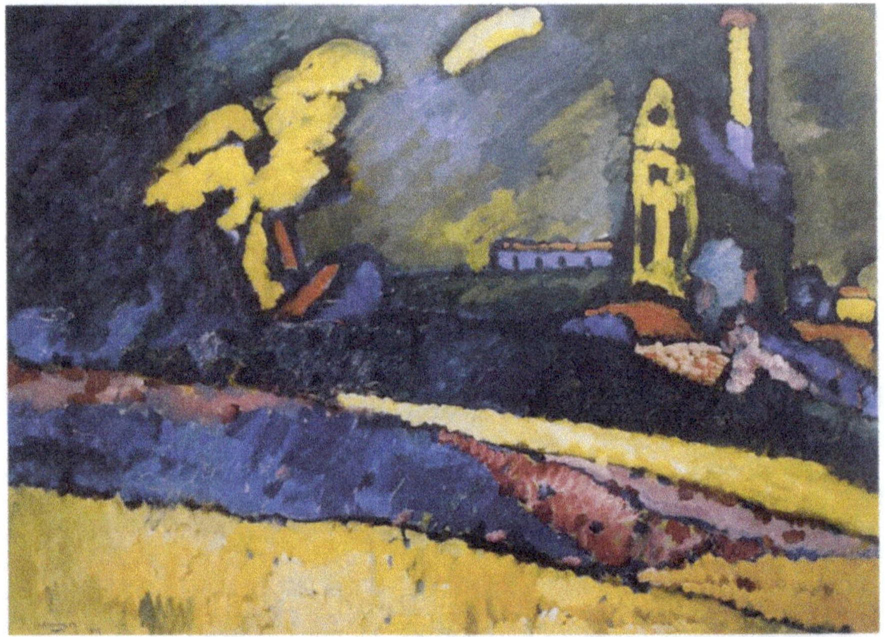

Figure 11.5 Vasily Kandinsky, *Murnau: Landscape with Church I*, 1909.

Private collection, Courtesy of Christie's, New York. © 1993 Christie's Images Limited. © 2022 Artists Rights Society (ARS), New York.

Galerie Neue Kunst, where Jawlensky's paintings were exhibited in August.

While in Munich Eddy purchased two paintings by the little-known Russian artist Genin, *Thirst* (*Durst*; Figure 11.8) and *Evening* (*Abend*), on August 19, 1913, from Thannhauser's Moderne Galerie.[4] The former depicts a female nude and the latter shows figures set against a landscape. At Max Dietzel's Kunstsalon, Eddy saw pictures on consignment by Franz Marc that he liked, but the prices were too high. So he waited until the following year to buy *Red Deer I* (*Rote Rehe I*; Figure 11.9) and *The Bewitched Mill* (*Die verzauberte Mühle*; Figure 11.10) directly from the artist. By then Kandinsky had also recommended Marc's work.

[4] I am grateful to Alexej Rodionov for his assistance. See Alexej Rodionov, "Lyrisches Element," and Ralph Jentsch, "Robert Genin und die Moderne Galerie Thannhauser in München" in *Robert Genin, 1884–1941: Russischer Expressionist in München*, exh. cat. (Murnau am Staffelsee, Germany: Schlossmuseum Murnau, 2018), 33, 82.

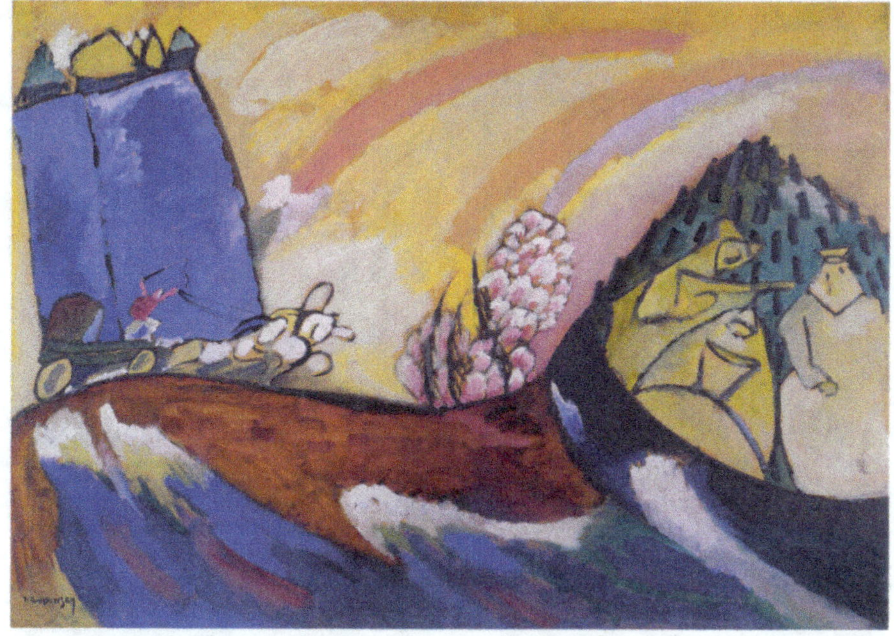

Figure 11.6 Vasily Kandinsky, *Painting with Troika*, 1911.

The Art Institute of Chicago: Arthur Jerome Eddy Memorial Collection (1931.509).

Eddy's letters to Kandinsky quoted above initiated a meaningful correspondence that provides insights into the collector's reasoning. Even though the two men never met, their letters reveal a lot about their opinions and personalities. On October 13, Eddy wrote again to Kandinsky:

> I have already bought more pictures than I can well afford, and I have more than I can hang to advantage, but the work of new men always tempts me. As a rule I do not buy the work of men who have arrived, that is who have so far succeeded that dealers are handling their pictures. It has been my good fortune to introduce, so to speak, some of our young American painters to the American public, that is to say I have bought their pictures when no one else would touch them, and after I had bought a few, then others became interested. It is the same old story of people waiting for somebody to take the lead, and of all people the dealers are the most timid. I have great respect and liking for a dealer like Durand-Ruel, who forty years ago risked his fortune and reputation in

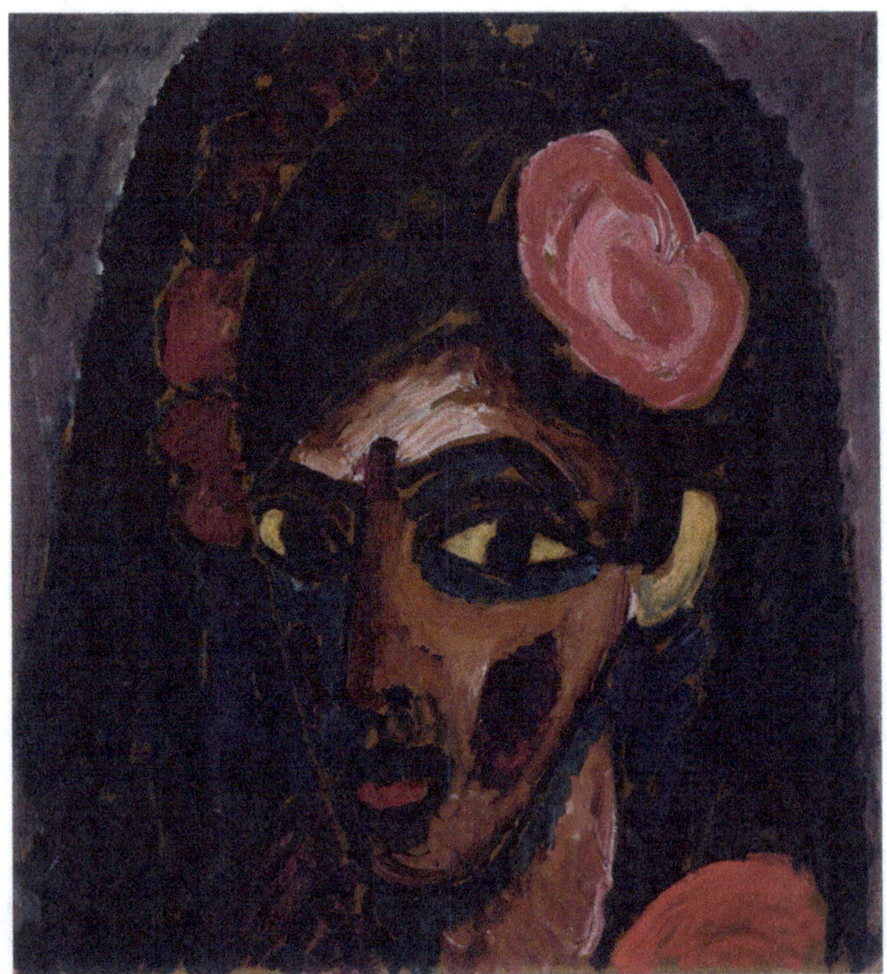

Figure 11.7 Alexei Jawlensky, *Egyptian Girl*, 1913.
Saint Louis Art Museum: Bequest of Morton D. May (897:1983).

supporting the leaders of the Impressionists. Now-a-days dealers seem to feel they are conferring a favor on the artist if they permit him to send his pictures to their galleries for sale on commission, a transaction in which the dealer takes no risk whatsoever, and yet claims the credit for "discovering" the artist.[5]

[5] Letter in English dated October 30, 1913, from Eddy to Kandinsky, Fonds Kandinsky, Musée National d'Art Moderne, Centre Georges Pompidou, Paris.

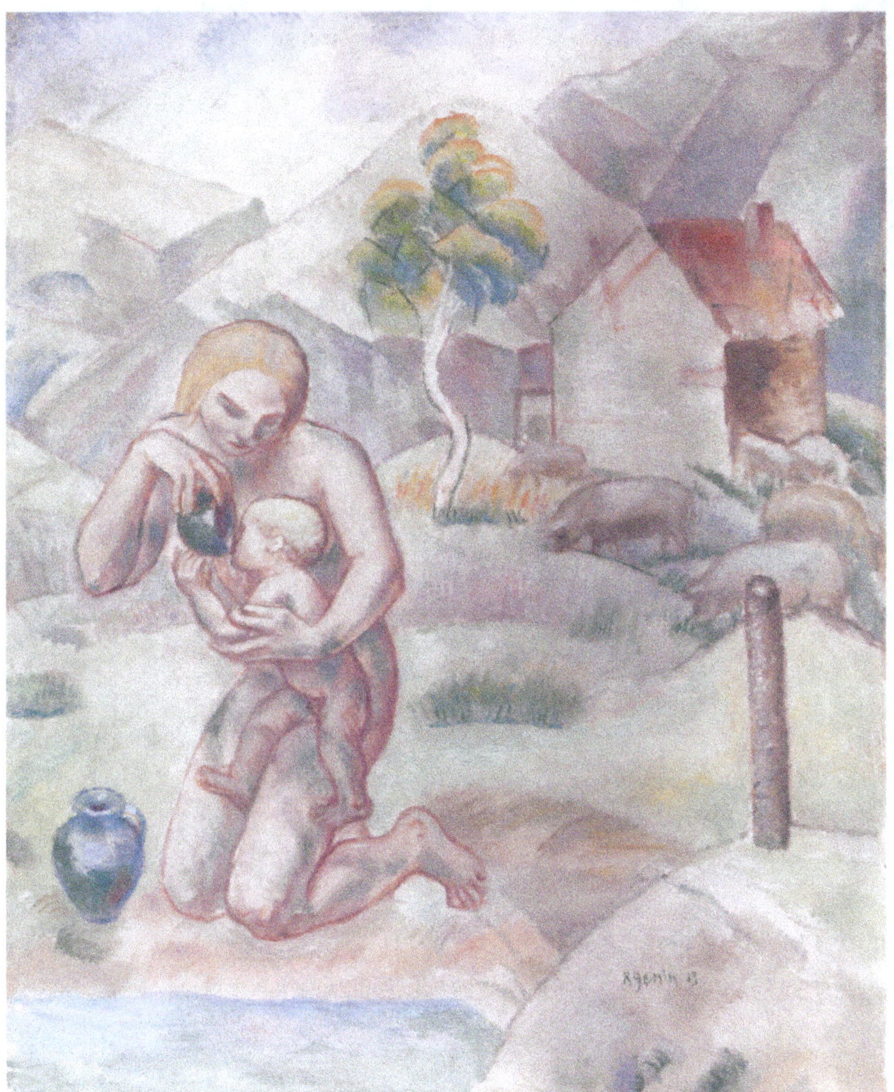

Figure 11.8 Robert Genin, *Thirst*, 1913.

The Art Institute of Chicago: Arthur Jerome Eddy Memorial Collection (1931.520)/Art Resource, NY.

In the same letter from October 30 he explained: "I enjoy the new art because it is so *vital*, and because I have the feeling that behind it there is a tremendous amount of sincerity and conviction." And he went on to say: "I congratulate Frau Kandinsky on not 'following in your footsteps in the realm of art', and in going her own way. …

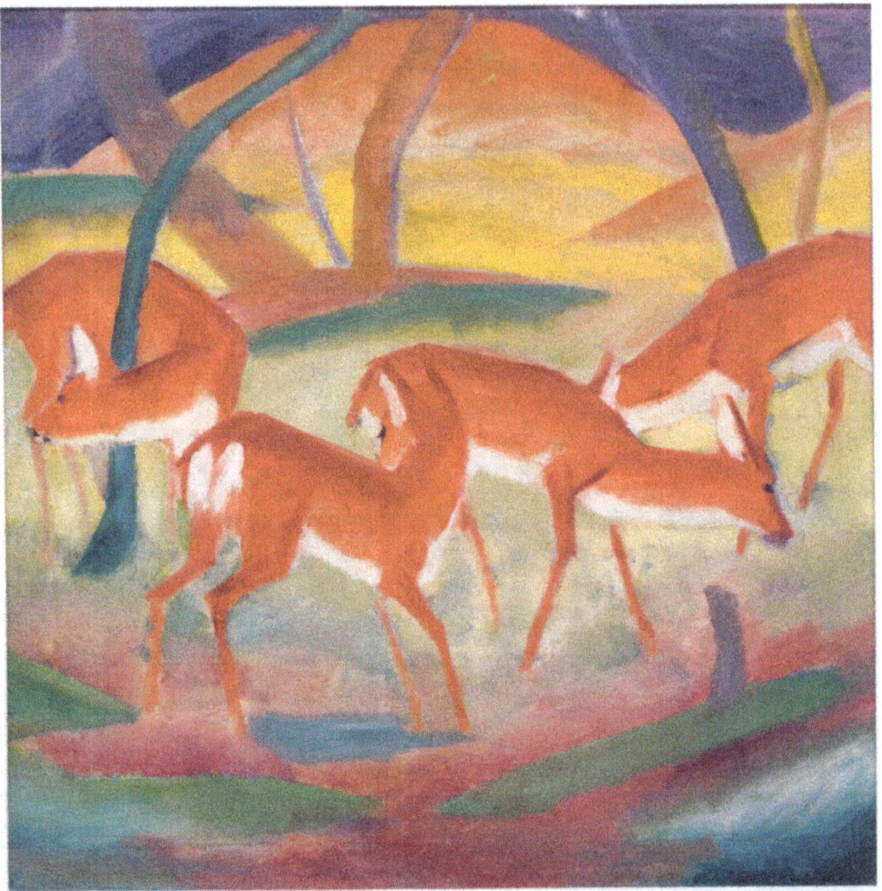

Figure 11.9 Franz Marc, *Red Deer I,* 1910–11.

Heidi Horten Collection, Vienna. Image courtesy of Heidi Horten Sammlung.

I would like very much to see something of her work, and I am going to make the following suggestion regarding some of the artists you named in your letter."

Kandinsky's letter of October 10, 1913, is lost, but in it he obviously mentioned Marc, Klee, Münter, Bloch, and Alfred Kubin because Eddy proceeded to ask Kandinsky to contact four of them on his behalf and make the following proposals: "Marc.—If he has a picture of about the size you mention, namely one square meter, which you and he consider fine, and he is willing to sell it for 400 marks, you may send it. Klee.— I do not buy etchings, but what you

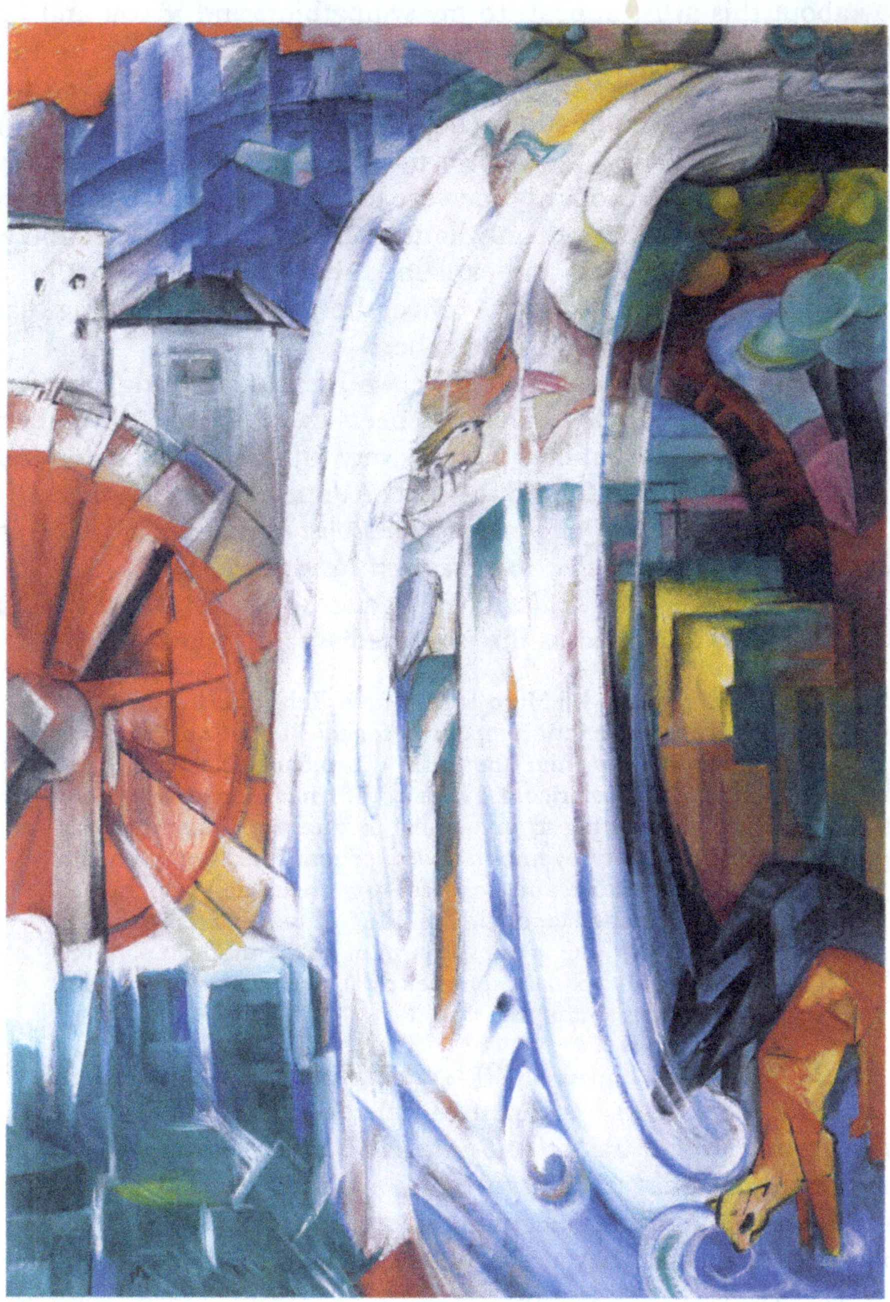

Figure 11.10 Franz Marc, *The Bewitched Mill*, 1913.

The Art Institute of Chicago: Arthur Jerome Eddy Memorial Collection (1931.522).

say about this artist appeals to my sympathies, and if you and he would select, say 4 or 5 of his etchings, at the best price he can consistently make, you may send them." In addition, he asked for two paintings by Münter (whom he referred to as "Frau Kandinsky") "at the best price she feels she can afford to make" and two by Bloch, although he thought they were too extreme for an American audience. Eddy stated "my only limitation in the way of selection is that I do not buy nudes" and explained that, since he hung all the pictures in his home and in his office, there could be nothing that might offend casual visitors and callers.[6]

Kandinsky soon contacted Marc, who reacted to Eddy's request in a letter to his colleague that has been dated to mid-November: "Eddy with his square meter prices is very unpleasant; I could send him the Red Deer for 400 and the Mill on approval for 600 [marks]." [*Eddy mit seinen □ mt [Quadratmeter] Preisen ist mir bedeutend unsympatischer; ich bleibe auch dabei, ihm die roten Rehe für 400 und die Mühle zur Ansicht für 600 zu senden.*][7] Eddy also wrote to Münter (who knew English and acted as the intermediary and translator):

> Of the two pictures by Marc I like "Rote Rehe" better than the "Muhle" [*sic*]. I have sent him a draft for the "Rote Rehe" and am waiting to hear from him about the two pictures. In your letter you did not quote a price if I kept both. I had hoped that Marc had sent one of his big strong animal pictures for I wanted a very characteristic picture by him in my collection. The "Rote Rehe" is a characteristic picture and possesses very great charm, but as yet I do not quite understand the "Mühle," that is it seems a little confused. However, the greatest charm of all the modern pictures is that they do not explain themselves at once, but reveal more and more on acquaintance.[8]

*Red Deer I* (see Figure 11.9) is approximately a square meter in size (87.6 × 88.3 cm) and features four deer set against a colorful background. In contrast, *The Bewitched Mill* (see Figure 11.10) contains multiple images dominated by a white waterfall. There are also birds flying, animals drinking water, and a red mill wheel. The painting was inspired by a trip the artist took to South Tyrol in late March 1913 to visit Maria Marc's father.

---

[6] All information comes from Eddy's letter dated October 30, 1913, to Kandinsky on the letterhead of the law offices of Eddy, Wetten & Pegler, The Temple, Chicago.

[7] Klaus Lankheit, ed., *Wassily Kandinsky-Franz Marc Briefwechsel* (Munich: R. Piper Verlag, 1983), 244–45.

[8] Letter in English, dated February 18, 1914, from Eddy to Münter, Gabriele Münter- und Johannes Eichner-Stiftung, Munich.

# XII

## Subsequent Purchases: Marc, Münter, Klee, and Bloch, 1914

Arthur Eddy purchased paintings by Franz Marc, Gabriele Münter, Paul Klee, and Albert Bloch only in 1914, when he also acquired more pictures by Kandinsky. According to Eddy's letter to Münter dated February 18, 1914, he purchased five of her pictures for 550 marks. Only two can be identified with existing works: *Still Life with Circle* (*Stilleben im Kreis*; Figure 12.1) and *Still Life with Queen* (*Stilleben mit Königin*; Figure 12.2). In this letter he explained: "I like your pictures very much indeed, they are all the more interesting because they do not seem to be influenced by your husband. You have an expression which is peculiarly your own." Eddy mentioned pictures with haystack and tree, houses in the woods, and a painting of masks in his correspondence; moreover, they appeared at the auction of his property in Chicago in 1937.[1]

Klee sent twenty-five works on paper to Eddy, who selected six tinted drawings that he purchased from the artist for 400 marks.[2] In his letter of April 29, Eddy told the artist: "I have tried to make the selection in such a way that the individual phases of your work are represented."[3] All attempts to trace the six drawings have been unsuccessful and they may have been destroyed. One, *Stonecutter II* (*Steinhauer II*; Figure 12.3), was illustrated in the *Blaue Reiter Almanach* (1912) edited by Kandinsky and Marc. Eddy reproduced another of Klee's drawings, *House by the Brook* (*Das Haus an der Brücke*), in *Cubists and Post-Impressionism,* where he wrote that: "There is another and almost unknown artist, P. Klee, who is very highly esteemed by the most advanced men. There is certainly an exquisite refinement to his line; it is so alive it scintillates."[4]

Eddy found Bloch's work to be "*most* interesting. It is exceedingly individual, and I find a great deal of pleasure in his very unusual use of color and also in the play of his imagination. I do not know of anything I can do for him further than purchase some of his pictures. ... I do not know why his people do not encourage

[1] Letter dated January 27, 1914, from Eddy to Mrs. Kandinsky and of March 5, 1914, to Kandinsky, Gabriele Münter- und Johannes Eichner-Stiftung, Munich. See the checklist for the auction at Williams, Barker & Severn Co., Chicago, January 20, 1937, nos. 104, 112, 180.

[2] Letter in English dated February 14, 1914, from Eddy to Klee and letter in German dated April 29, 1914, from Eddy to Klee sent to Kandinsky's Munich address are preserved in the Archive of the Zentrum Paul Klee, Bern, Switzerland.

[3] English translation in Michael Baumgartner, "The Beginnings: Paul Klee and America before 1920" in *Klee and America*, exh. cat. (Houston, TX: The Menil Collection, 2006), 28n20.

[4] Arthur Jerome Eddy, *Cubists and Post-Impressionism* (Chicago: A. C. McClurg & Co., 1914), 114 and illustration opposite p. 88.

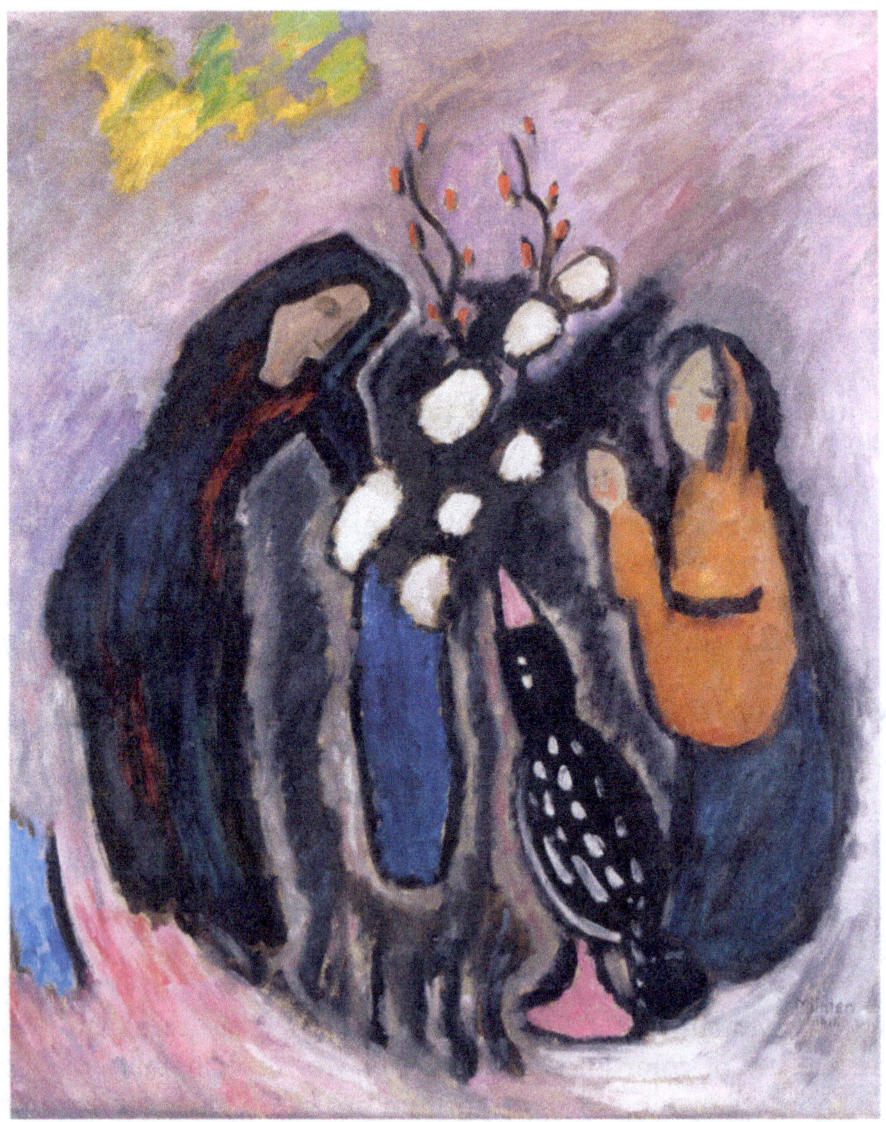

Figure 12.1 Gabriele Münter, *Still Life with Circle*, 1911.

Private collection, courtesy of Ketterer Kunst, Munich. 

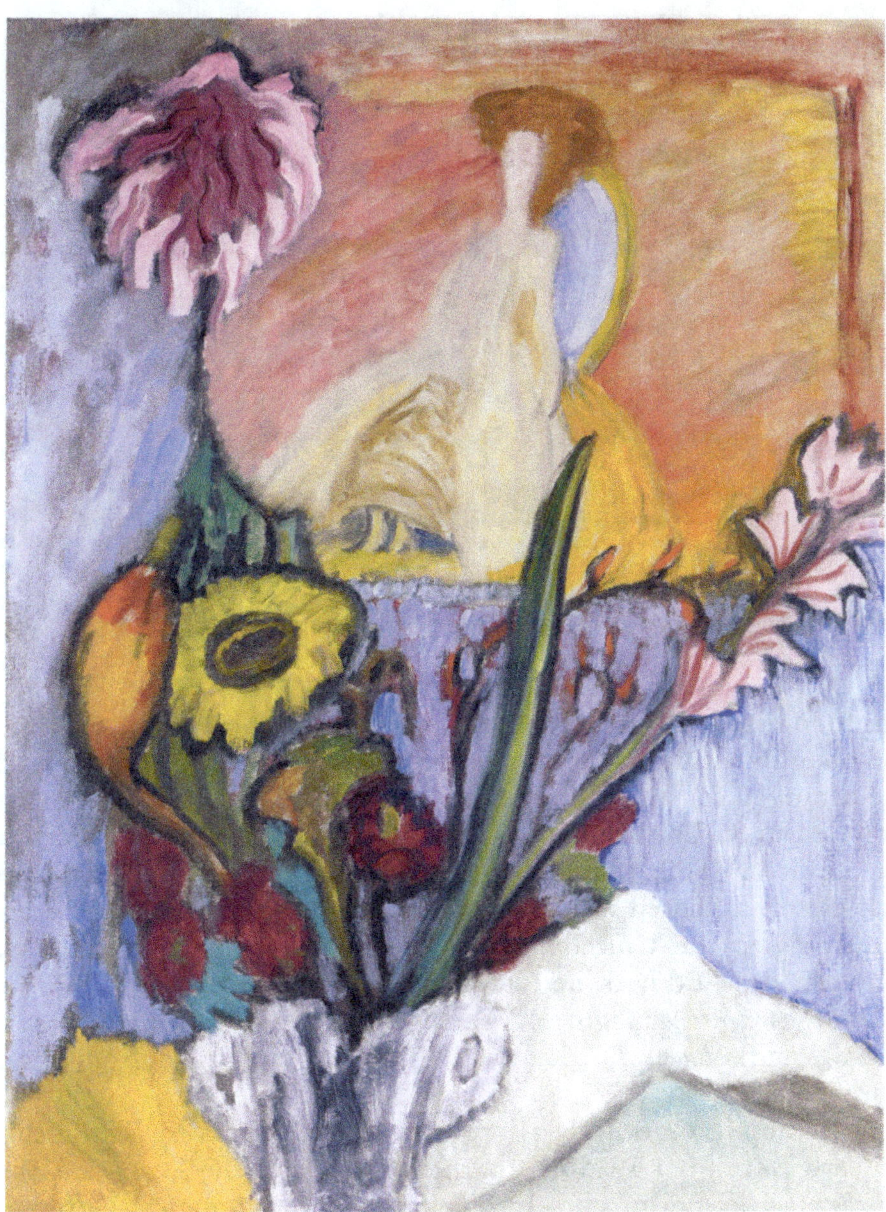

Figure 12.2 Gabriele Münter, *Still Life with Queen*, 1912.

The Art Institute of Chicago: Arthur Jerome Eddy Memorial Collection (1931.521). 

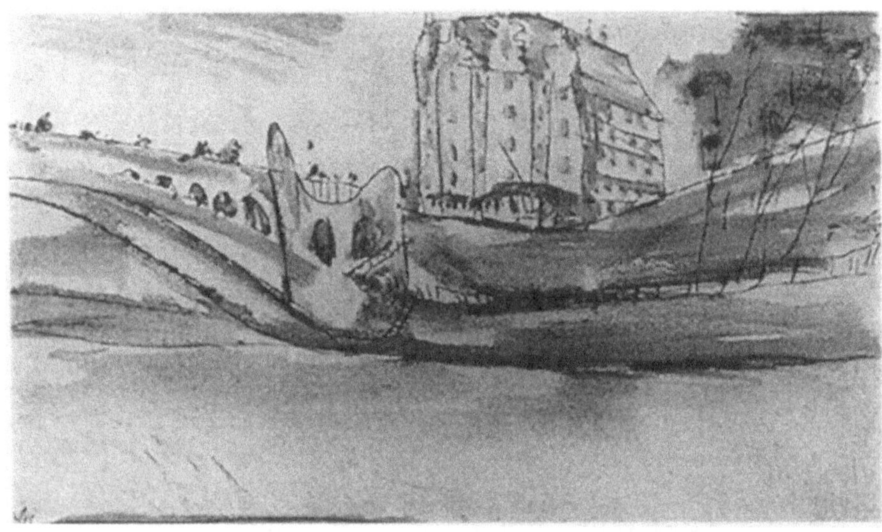

Figure 12.3 Paul Klee, *Stonecutter II*, 1910.

Location unknown. Image courtesy Zentrum Paul Klee, Bern.

his following art. I shall do whatever I can to aid him."[5] At the time he bought paintings—among them *Night*—and, the following year, he arranged for an exhibition at the Art Institute of Chicago that traveled to St. Louis. Albert Bloch was an American artist, born in St. Louis in 1882, who went to Europe at the end of 1908 and was closely affiliated with the Blaue Reiter group in Munich. After returning to the United States in 1921, he settled in Lawrence, Kansas. In all Eddy owned about twenty of his paintings: *Summer Night* (*Sommernacht*; Figure 12.4), *Night I* (*Nacht I*), *Lamentation* (*Klagelied*), and *Clowns II* (*Clownbild II*) having been acquired at an early date.

Arthur Jerome Eddy also owned twenty works by Kandinsky. In early December 1913 he saw the catalogue of the *Erster Deutscher Herbstsalon* in Berlin and, in a letter in ungrammatical German, offered Kandinsky 400 marks for his canvas *Landscape with Red Spots II* (*Landschaft mit roten Flecken*; Figure 12.5).[6] The painting had ar-

[5] Letter in English dated March 5, 1914, from Eddy to Kandinsky, Gabriele Münter- und Johannes Eichner-Stiftung, Munich.

[6] Letter in German dated December 8, 1913, from Eddy in New York to Kandinsky, Wassily Kandinsky Papers, Special Collections, The Getty Research Institute, Los Angeles. Text of letter published in Vivian Endicott Barnett, "Kandinsky Collectors in America, 1913–1930," in *Vasily Kandinsky: From Blaue Reiter to the Bauhaus, 1910–1925*, exh. cat. (New York: Neue Galerie, 2013), 91.

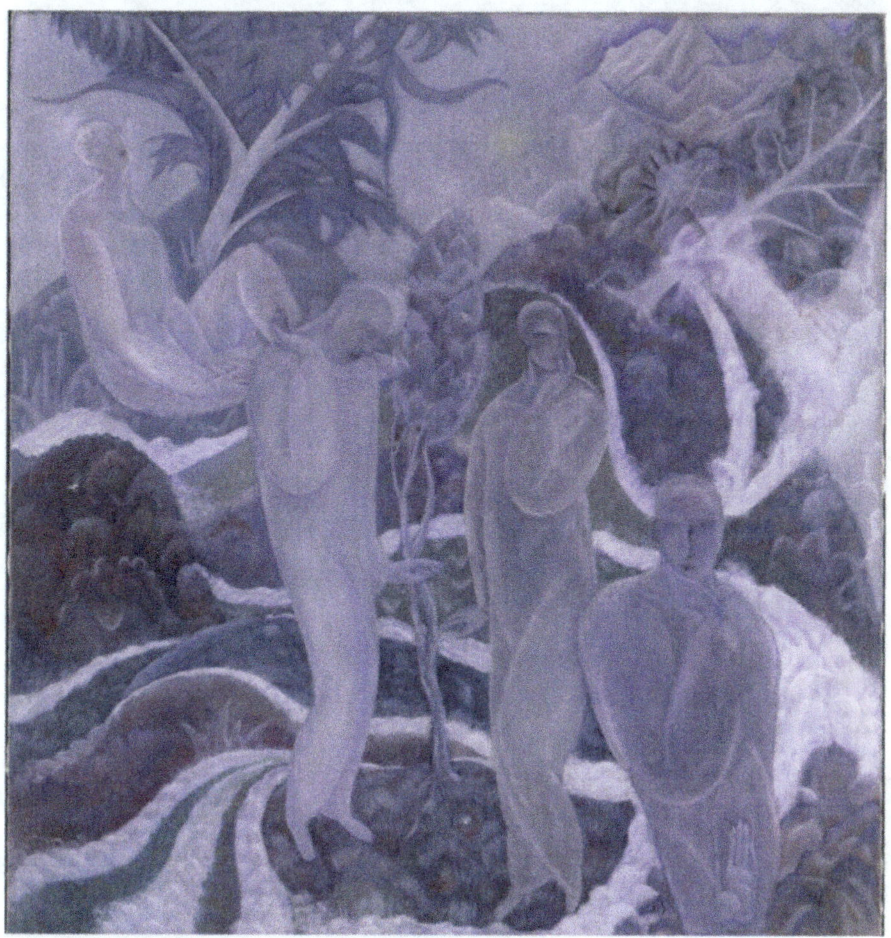

Figure 12.4 Albert Bloch, *Summer Night*, 1913.



rived in Chicago by March and Eddy wrote the artist that: "In many respects I think it is better than any other picture of yours which I have. It is certainly a very fine composition. It is brilliant and beautiful in color. I had a very distinguished Japanese expert at my house last evening and he enjoyed your pictures very much."[7] In this letter

[7] Letter in English dated March 5, 1914, from Eddy to Kandinsky, Gabriele Münter- und Johannes Eichner-Stiftung, Munich. Although the Japanese expert is not named, he was probably Chō Yō.

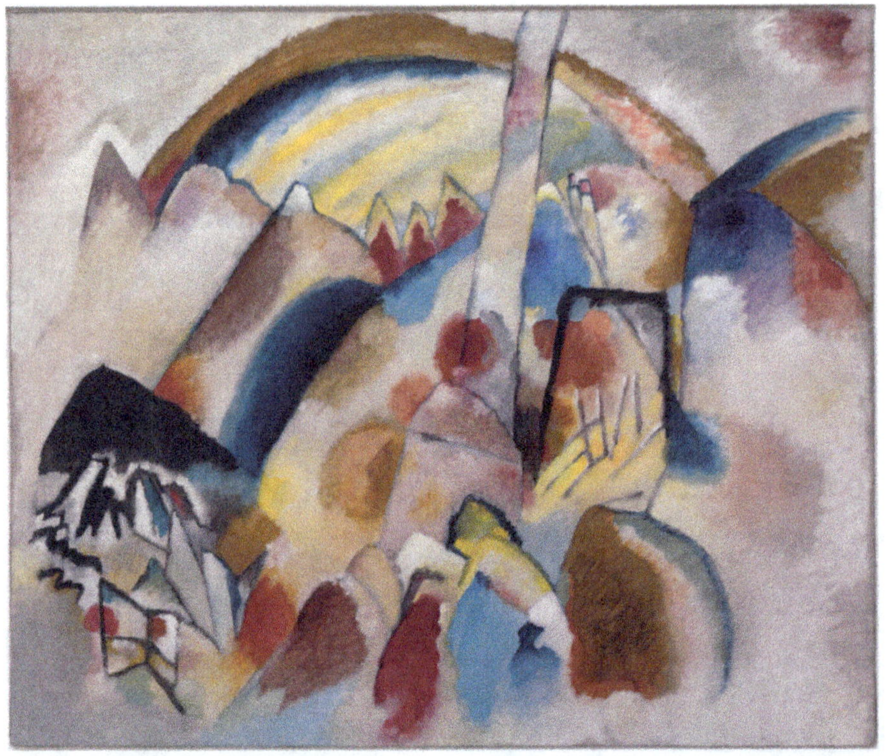

Figure 12.5 Vasily Kandinsky, *Landscape with Red Spots II* (*Landschaft mit roten Flecken, Nr. 2*), 1913.

Peggy Guggenheim Collection, Venice (Solomon R. Guggenheim Foundation, New York) 76.2553 PG 033.

Eddy mentions that the same person liked Bloch's *Night,* Marc's *Red Deer,* Münter's *Still Life with Queen* and *Masks,* as well as Klee's drawings.

On May 19, 1914, Eddy wrote again to Kandinsky that he might be in Europe during the summer and, if so, "shall try to run down to Munich. If you happen to be away, perhaps, I could see what pictures are in your studio just as I did last year. … If I do not go to Europe, and feel that I can afford to purchase any more of your pictures, I may write you to send over six or eight of your latest and most brilliant pictures, and I would keep two or three of those that I like, but I should want you to make me a much better price than 600 marks, because you must realize that I cannot afford to buy so many pictures of one artist unless the price is very low. It is not like buying one picture where it does not make much difference whether you pay 100 marks more or less, but having as many of your pictures as I have I ought not to buy any more, and would not think of doing so if I did not enjoy your work very much indeed."[8]

Two months later he had not left for Europe. After receiving the *Kandinsky 1901–1913 Album* published by Der Sturm in Berlin, Eddy wrote to Münter: "I thought I was nearly through buying pictures this year, but if he [Kandinsky] cares to make a *very special* price on three of the pictures referred to in his letter, I will take them ... for one thousand marks."[9] Thus, Eddy purchased his last works by Kandinsky just before the outbreak of World War I: *Painting with Green Center* (*Bild mit grüner Mitte*; Figure 12.6), *Improvisation with Red and Blue Ring* (*Improvisation mit rot-blauem Ring*), and *Little Painting with Yellow* (*Kleines Bild mit Gelb*; Figure 12.7). He did not go to Europe again, even after the Great War ended in 1918. Nevertheless, his correspondence with Kandinsky and Münter did not end.

Although the two men never met, Eddy revealed more to Kandinsky through Münter than he had to many other people. The language barrier vanished as he had explained to Münter earlier: "I am writing in English, because I met an artist, Mr. Hartley, in New York, and he told me that you speak very good English, therefore you must write to me in English. Think of the advantage we will have over Herr Kandinsky who does not read English. We can say anything we please about his pictures!"[10] Eddy relied on Kandinsky for advice about which Munich artists' work to buy. He also described to Kandinsky his new pattern for collecting by buying several works at a low price directly from the artist. He drove a hard bargain, which annoyed Marc and would later alienate some American artists.

When he first began to collect, Eddy bought from art galleries—such as O'Brien in Chicago or Durand-Ruel in Paris—and turned to artists for portrait commissions. Many of the works he acquired at the Armory Show were lent by the artists themselves, although the paintings by Derain and Vlaminck came from the Paris dealer Daniel-Henry Kahnweiler. During the summer of 1913 Eddy

[8] Letter in English dated May 19, 1914, from Eddy to Kandinsky, Gabriele Münter- und Johannes Eichner-Stiftung, Munich.
[9] Letter in English dated July 18, 1914 from Eddy to Münter, Gabriele Münter-und Johannes Eichner-Stiftung, Munich.
[10] Letter in English dated Jan. 27, 1914 from Eddy to Mrs. Kandinsky, Gabriele Münter-und Johannes Eichner-Stiftung, Munich.

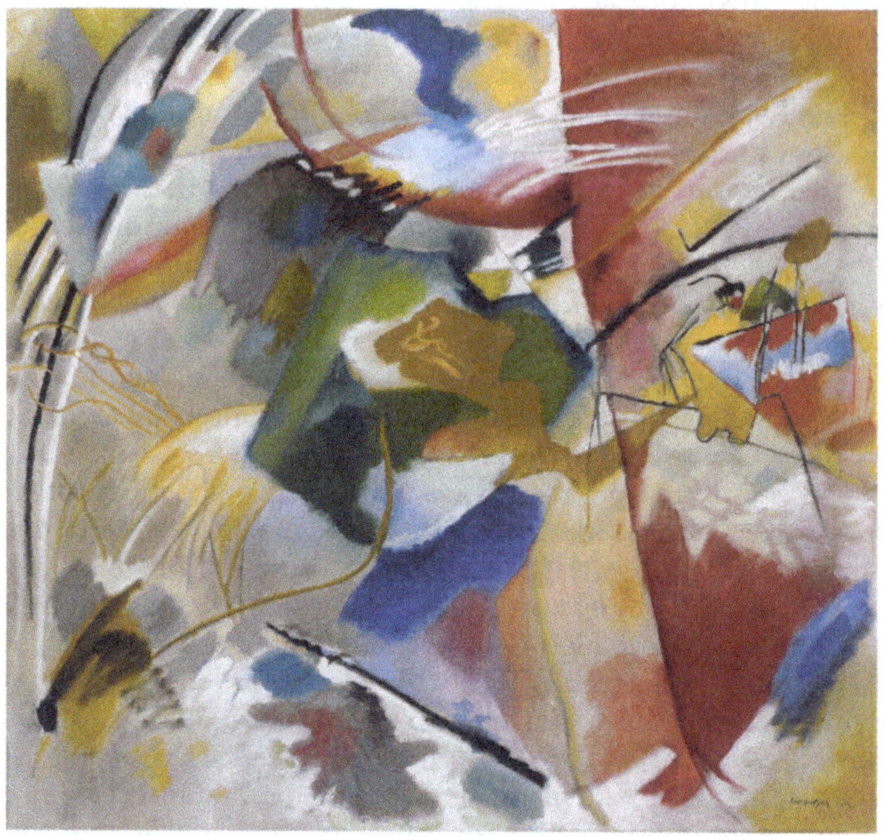

Figure 12.6 Vasily Kandinsky, *Painting with Green Center*, 1913.
The Art Institute of Chicago: Arthur Jerome Eddy Memorial Collection (1931.510).

purchased paintings directly from Kandinsky and Jawlensky, thereby shifting to a new strategy. Although Eddy realized that there were advantages for an artist to be represented by a prominent gallery, he admired Whistler's contempt for art dealers. As he related to Kandinsky, "Whistler had a positive dislike for dealers, and if he had transactions with them he nearly always fell out with them. ... [and] to the end of his days he would have as little to do with them, as he could. To me the attitude of the average dealer is positively distasteful, because he does not hesitate to urge upon a buyer, as a masterpiece, some picture which he knows is a very inferior work of the artist." Citing his visit to Kahnweiler's gallery and a Derain

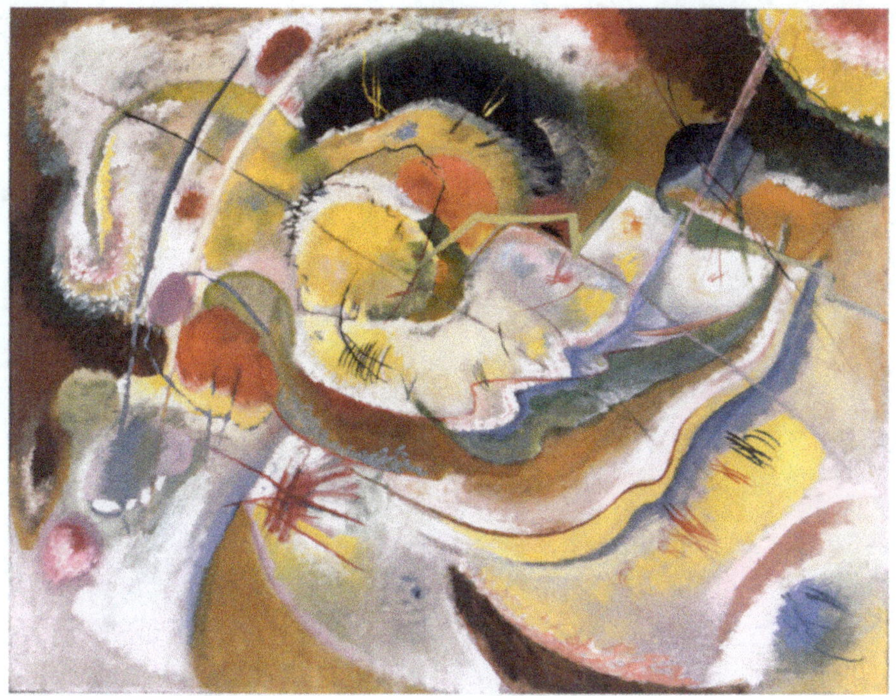

Figure 12.7 Vasily Kandinsky, *Little Painting with Yellow* (*Improvisation*), 1914.

Philadelphia Museum of Art: The Louise and Walter Arensberg Collection, 1950 (1950-134-103).


painting that the dealer was promoting, Eddy wrote that "I would be very sorry for any man who happened to buy the Derain he showed me."[11]

[11] Letter in English dated October 30, 1913, from Eddy to Kandinsky, Fonds Kandinsky, Musée National d'Art Moderne, Centre Georges Pompidou, Paris.

# XIII

## *Cubists and Post-Impressionism*, 1914

Before his trip to Europe, undoubtedly inspired by the Armory Show, Arthur Eddy was writing a book. In May 1913 the society columnist for the *Chicago Daily Tribune* reported that he was working on a book to come out in the autumn and provided the actual title.[1] On September 23 that year, Eddy wrote Kandinsky: "The book I am just finishing will probably appear this winter. … It will give me great pleasure to send you a copy when the book comes out. I think it will be the most authoritative thing in English for some time to come."[2] Two months later he told Kandinsky: "I particularly enjoy the way your letters are written and your manner of expressing yourself in writing. You will find quite a little of your writings both printed in articles and letters contained in my book which will probably come out before the first of March."[3] *Cubists and Post-Impressionism* was published in March 1914 by A. C. McClurg. The first chapter, titled "A Sensation," states that since the exhibit at the Columbian Exposition, "nothing has happened in the world of American art so stimulating as the recent INTERNATIONAL EXHIBITION OF MODERN ART." Eddy emphasizes the word *stimulating* and the *severe jolt* that the show gave to American art.[4] He writes: "I would like to own Raphaels and Titians and Rembrandts and Velasquezes, but I can't afford it … [yet] their paintings belong to the world and should be in public places for the enjoyment and instruction of *all*. It is the high privilege of the private buyer to buy the works of *new men*."[5] Frequently he quotes excerpts from books by Théodore Duret and Frank Rutter among others; most pages have footnotes citing articles in periodicals.

The second chapter focuses on Post-Impressionism and includes a discussion of the origins of Impressionism in order to explain what came after—and where Whistler fits in. Without naming Bertha Palmer, he writes that: "One of the early buyers of Impressionist pictures was a distinguished Chicago woman, and her collection today contains some of the finest Monets, Renoirs, and Degases in existence." He went on to explain that her friends couldn't understand why she bought Monet, and now, less than

[1] Mme X, "News of the Society World," *Chicago Daily Tribune*, May 25, 1913, F3.

[2] Letter in English dated September 23, 1913, from Eddy to Kandinsky, Wassily Kandinsky Papers, Special Collections, The Getty Research Institute, Los Angeles.

[3] Letter in English dated November 24, 1913, from Eddy to Kandinsky, Wassily Kandinsky Papers, Special Collections, The Getty Research Institute, Los Angeles.

[4] Arthur Jerome Eddy, *Cubists and Post-Impressionism* (Chicago: A. C. McClurg & Co., 1914), 1–3.

[5] Eddy, *Cubists*, 5–6.

thirty years later, the pictures are worth ten, fifteen, twenty times what they originally cost.[6] Although Eddy bought two Manets and a Monet, he did not acquire them in large numbers or spend large sums of money. After all, these artists had been discovered and their paintings were sold by major art galleries for good prices.

In the third chapter, titled "Les Fauves," he writes at length about Paul Cézanne, Paul Gauguin, and Vincent van Gogh, although they are generally considered to be Post-Impressionists. He does get to Henri Matisse and lists Odilon Redon and Kees van Dongen among numerous other Fauves. Probably for the same reason that he didn't own Raphaels or Rembrandts, Eddy did not collect works by Cézanne, Gauguin, Van Gogh, or Matisse. The only pictures by Fauve artists in his collection were the Derain and the Vlaminck that he purchased at the Armory Show; however, he discusses them, respectively, in relation to Cubism and Virile-Impressionism. Although he does not mention Émilie Charmy, her painting of L'Estaque belongs with the Fauves. Eddy defines *Fauvism* as meaning "a mood rather than a mode."[7] In writing about Matisse, he quotes an interview printed in the *New York Times* on March 9, 1913. He reproduces in color the picture by Dove in his own collection and publishes what Dove wrote to him about it. The chapter concludes by citing an exhibition that took place at the MacDowell Club in New York the previous November with works by Konrad Cramer, Andrew Dasburg, and William Zorach; thus proving that he added to the book after his trip to Europe.

The following three chapters are devoted to modern art in general and Cubism in particular. He does not advocate Cubism or any other "ism" in either art or life. Rather, Eddy pleads for "*tolerance and intelligent receptivity*, for an attitude of sympathetic appreciation toward *everything that is new and strange and revolutionary in life*."[8] Relying on Guillaume Apollinaire's *Les peintres cubistes* of 1913, he traces the history of Cubism and its various tendencies by citing paintings in his collection that are reproduced: Duchamp's *King and Queen* and *Chess Players* as well as Picabia's *Dances at the Source.* He reproduces Gleizes's *Man on a Balcony* as the frontispiece, states that visitors to the Armory Show liked it best of all because it looked like a painting of a man in armor, and concludes that "appreciation

[6] Eddy, *Cubists*, 27.
[7] Eddy, *Cubists*, 47.
[8] Eddy, *Cubists*, 65.

is largely a matter of association rather than knowledge and taste." Eddy proposes that "on its technical side, Cubism is simply a systematic use of planes."[9] As in his earlier publications, Eddy seeks to define the subject at hand and relies upon excerpts from recent publications by critics to argue his case.

The chapter on the "New Art in Munich" reflects his visit there during the summer of 1913 and his subsequent correspondence with Kandinsky. Eddy quotes from the letters (now lost) that he received from the artist about the designation of the cannons in *Improvisation 30* and how the artist's paintings from the past fifteen years come from within.[10] Eddy paraphrases Kandinsky's text "On the Question of Form," which was published in the *Blaue Reiter Almanach* in May 1912, as well as *Über das Geistige in der Kunst* (*On the Spiritual in Art*). His information about the New Artists' Association of Munich comes from Otto Fischer's *Das Neue Bild* as do other citations. At the back of Eddy's book, there is an extensive bibliography of recent publications organized by language (English, French, German). It seems impossible that an active attorney could have consulted so many art historical sources, and it is not known who compiled the bibliography and assisted with his research.

Additional chapters discuss Alexander W. Rimington's color organ, Henry P. Bowie's writings on Japanese painting and esoragoto, and also the Futurist manifesto. Eddy did not collect any works by the Italian Futurists. Neither did he own Cubist paintings by Picasso, Georges Braque, Robert Delaunay, and Fernand Léger. The chapter on American art, which he calls "Virile-Impressionism," mentions not only Homer and Kroll, but also John Singer Sargent, Robert Henri, and Arthur Davies, whose art is not represented in Eddy's collection. He extends the term *Virile-Impressionism* to include landscapes by the European artists Segonzac and Souza Cardoso.

A short chapter on sculpture refers to Constantin Brancusi, whose work was considered earlier in the book in relation to Futurism, where Eddy wrote that "I have a golden bronze head—a 'Sleeping Muse' by Brancusi" and quotes Roger Fry writing in *The Nation* in August on Brancusi at the Allied Artists' Exhibition in London.[11] Eddy illustrates sculptures that he did not own by Brancusi, Matisse, and Wilhelm Lehmbruck. There is a short chapter titled "In Conclu-

---

[9] Eddy, *Cubists*, 72.
[10] Eddy, *Cubists*, 125–26, 130–31.
[11] Eddy, *Cubists*, 182–83.

sion" in which Eddy categorizes Superficial Impressionism (Monet), Realistic Impressionism (Manet), and Substantial Impressionism (Cézanne), but does not conclude anything about Cubism or Post-Impressionism, the subject of his book. The last chapters and two appendixes seem to have been written hastily. Eddy probably drafted most of the six chapters dealing with Post-Impressionism and the Cubists and decided after his trip to Europe to add chapters VII through XIV. He added a few details to an earlier section of the manuscript: for example, a footnote about Arnold Schönberg's music having been performed in Chicago on December 31, 1913.[12]

On May 19, 1914, Eddy wrote to Kandinsky: "You will both be pleased to know that the book is meeting with a more favorable reception than any of us expected. I think that in another year there will be quite a little interest in the new art in America. Already one or two New York dealers wish to have exhibitions of some of the extreme modern pictures."[13] One person who was not pleased with the book was John Quinn. In a personal letter to Mitchell Kennerly dated April 12, 1914, he wrote that the book "is monstrous. Horrible on the outside; cheeky as hell on the inside; conceited, laughable; just what you would expect from a Chicago 'ass-pirant.'"[14] Eddy's friend Harriet Monroe mentioned the book in the *Chicago Daily Tribune* in April; the *New York Times* published a lengthy, anonymous review in June; and *The Little Review* followed in July.[15] There is no indication of how Kandinsky or Münter may have reacted to the book and there is surprisingly little recorded response by American artists. Georgia O'Keeffe is known to have perused Eddy's book. The educator Alon Bemont advised her to get *Cubists and Post-Impressionism* and *On the Spiritual in Art*. She recalled: "He told me to look at the pictures in Eddy's book—that I needn't bother to read it—but that I should read the Kandinsky. I looked at the Eddy

[12] Eddy, *Cubists*, 9.

[13] Letter in English dated May 19, 1914, from Eddy to Kandinsky, Gabriele Münter- und Johannes Eichner-Stiftung, Munich.

[14] Letter dated April 12, 1914, from John Quinn to Mitchell Kennerly, John Quinn Papers, Manuscript and Archives Division, The New York Public Library, Letter book 7, 616–17.

[15] Harriet Monroe, "'Modernism' in Art a Popular Subject," *Chicago Daily Tribune*, April 5, 1914, G8; "Art at Home and Abroad: Cubists, Post-Impressionists and Other Rebels Against the Conventional in Painting Analyzed in New Book," *New York Times*, June 21, 1914, SM10; and Alexander Kaun, "The 'Savage' Painters," *The Little Review* I, no. 5 (July 1914): 63.

very carefully and I read the Kandinsky."[16] She was particularly struck by the color reproduction of Dove's *Based on Leaf Forms and Spaces* that Eddy had purchased in 1912.

[16] See William Innes Homer, *Alfred Stieglitz and the American Avant-Garde* (Boston: New York Graphic Society, 1977), 236; and Debra Bricker Balken, *Dove/O'Keeffe: Circles of Influence*, exh. cat. (Williamstown, MA: Sterling and Francine Clark Art Institute, 2009), 21.

# XIV

## Joseph Müller and Edwin Campbell, 1914

By the time Eddy's book came out, his enthusiasm and influence were communicated to other collectors. In May 1914 he arranged for Edwin R. Campbell to commission Kandinsky to paint four panels for the foyer of Campbell's new apartment at 635 Park Avenue in New York. Eddy had known Campbell for many years: They both had lived in Flint, Michigan (but not during the same years); they shared an early fascination with automobiles; they had second homes in Pasadena; and their wives were cousins.[1] On May 21 Eddy wrote from the Hotel Gotham to Kandinsky in Munich: "I have persuaded a friend here in New York to buy some of your work. He is taking the pictures entirely upon my urging him to do so and therefor [*sic*] I am very anxious they shall please him and his wife when they are in his home. He wants four paintings for the four walls of a reception hall. ... I like, of all the pictures I have of yours, the 'Landschaft mit rotem flachen [*sic*]' the best, it is so brilliant in color that it makes a beautiful wall decoration. Now I think my friend would like four pictures painted in the same mood, strong brilliant pictures. The four should be in the same mood so that they will harmonize and make four beautiful walls. ... But you are to use your own judgmend [*sic*]."[2] Eddy provided dimensions, a description of the entry hall and its furnishings, suggestions on how to frame the panels, and enclosed a pencil sketch (Figure 14.1).[3] In the same letter he added: "I was glad to get this commission for Herr Kandinsky because it gives him an entrance in New York, and while the price is not large, yet it is quite a venture for my friend to hang four such extremely modern pictures in a place where everybody must see them. I think my friend has a good deal of courage, but I am very sure he will be very much pleased with the result. I am sure Kandinsky will choose a beautiful color scheme." In fact, only one of the Campbell panels has really brilliant colors (Figure 14.2) and Kandinsky chose a different palette for each of the panels so that they were mistakenly thought to represent the four seasons.

---

[1] For more information, see Vivian Endicott Barnett, "Kandinsky Collectors in America, 1913–1930," in *Vasily Kandinsky: From Blaue Reiter to the Bauhaus, 1910–1925*, exh. cat. (New York: Neue Galerie, 2013), 94–96.

[2] Letter in English dated May 21, 1914, from Eddy to Kandinsky, Gabriele Münter- und Johannes Eichner-Stiftung, Munich.

[3] Letter in English dated June 15, 1914, from Eddy to Münter, Gabriele Münter- und Johannes Eichner-Stiftung, Munich.

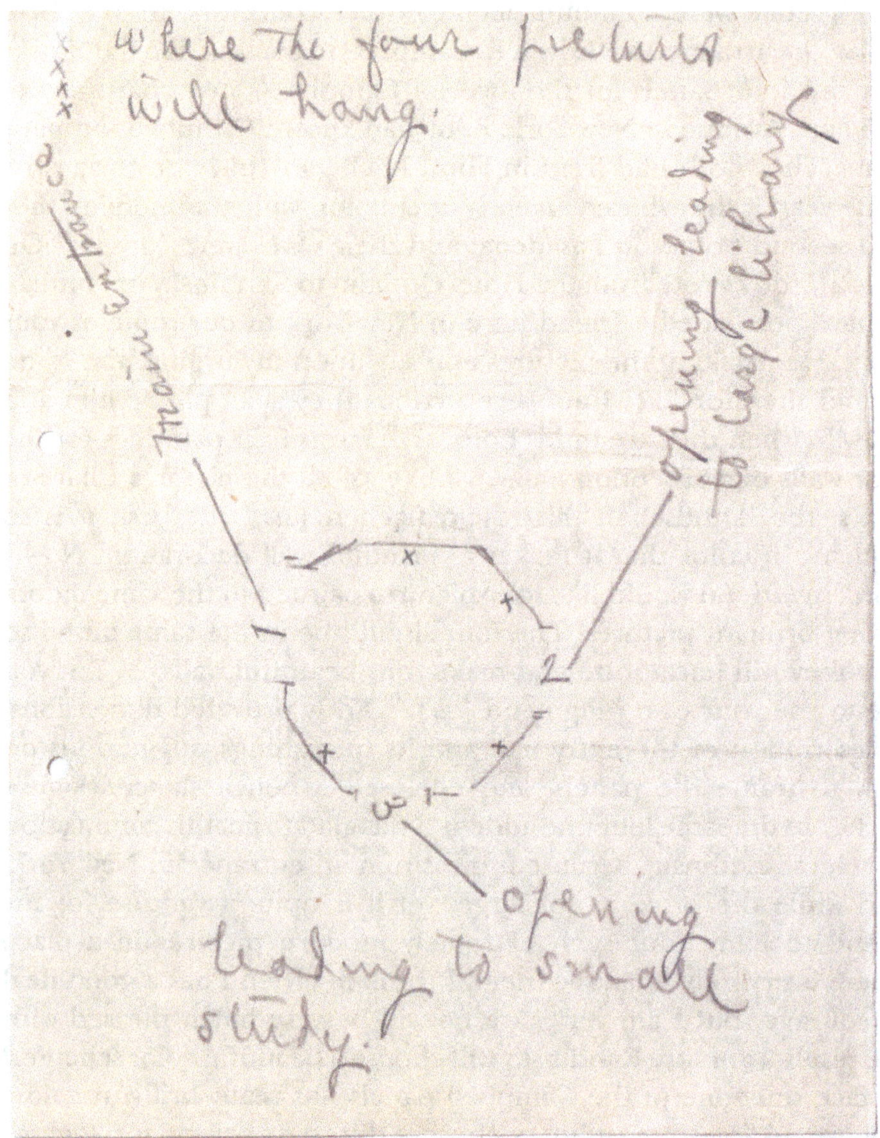


Figure 14.1 Arthur Jerome Eddy, *Sketch of reception hall in Campbell apartment* in letter of June 15, 1914.

Gabriele Münter- und Johannes Eichner-Stiftung, Munich.

Because of the war, the works of art could not be shipped to New York from Germany. Eddy advised Münter—and also Bloch—to send paintings by way of Genoa, specifying an agent there. However,

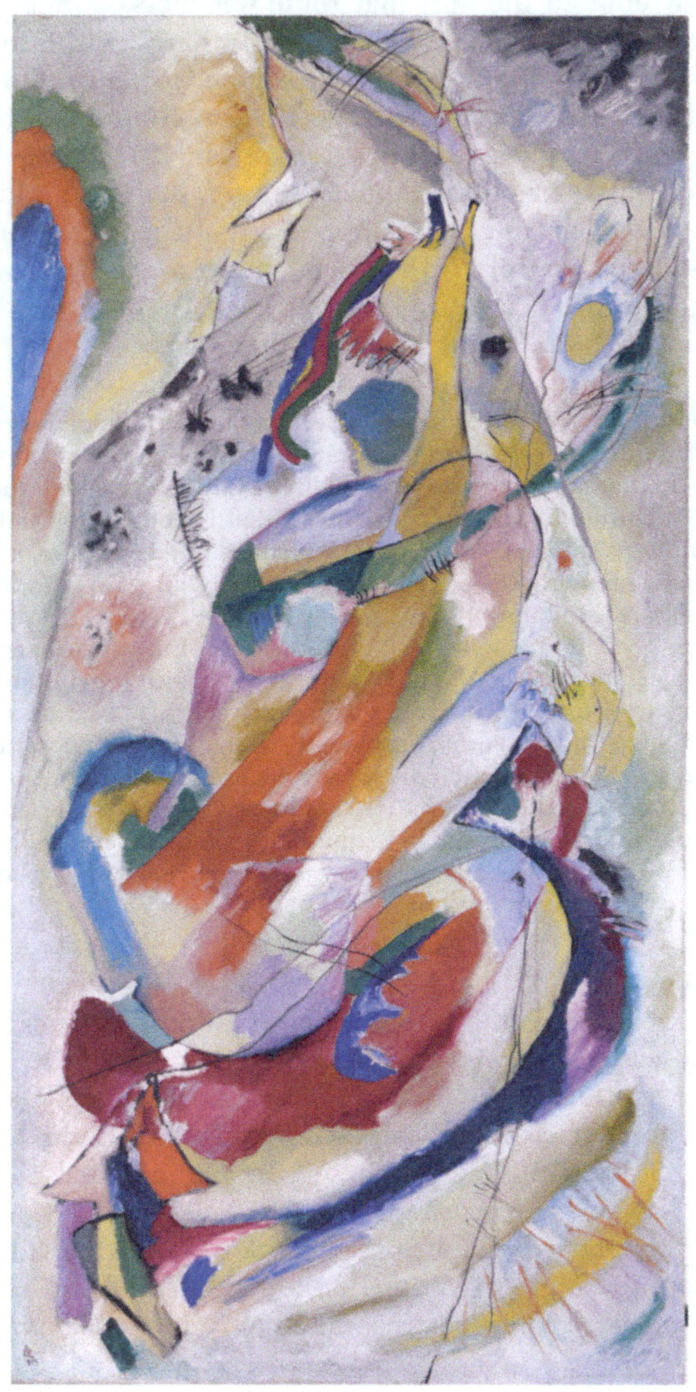

Figure 14.2 Vasily Kandinsky, *Panel for Edwin R. Campbell, No. 1*, 1914.

The Museum of Modern Art, New York: Mrs. Simon Guggenheim Fund. Digital image © The Museum of Modern Art/Licensed by SCALA/Art Resource, NY. © 2022 Artists Rights Society (ARS), New York.

once Italy entered the war, that route was blocked. Subsequently the Campbell panels made their way to Amsterdam with the Dutch collector Willem Beffie and were then shipped to neutral Stockholm. Throughout 1913 Eddy continued to write to Münter regarding the panels, which finally arrived in New York in 1916. From Sweden, where Kandinsky had gone to meet Münter, she sent on his behalf a proposal "which, can be, I suppose, advantageous to both of us: these three years 1916, 17, 18 I oblige myself to send you two of my *best* new paintings of the size of about 1 square meter for the price of 600 dollars both."[4] Eddy declined the offer:

> I cannot very well agree to take a certain number of pictures each year. I do not like to do that because I buy more pictures than I should. I always like to see the pictures I buy before taking them. When I wrote in my letter to Moscow that I thought it would be good for you to have some of your pictures in this country, it was because I thought the pictures were doing you no good in Europe. If you are exhibiting the pictures in Europe they will do you as much good there as if they were over here. But if you have no more exhibitions coming in Europe, and you wish to send me six or eight pictures I would be glad to see them, and would hold them here for you. Perhaps somebody might buy one. Or perhaps there might be an exhibition of your pictures in this country later on. ... Of course, your pictures ought to bring higher prices in Europe than in this country, because they are better known there. In this country they are not known at all, except by the people who have seen mine.[5]

In August 1914, Josef Müller, a young Swiss collector who was completing an internship in the United States and whose trip around the world was cut short by the war, visited Eddy's home in Chicago, where he saw Kandinsky's paintings for the first time. Deeply impressed, he contacted the Galerie Der Sturm in Berlin upon his return to Switzerland and purchased the monumental *Composition V* of 1911 as well as *Improvisation 31* (*Sea Battle*) of 1913. At Eddy's home he would have seen the preceding works from the same series, *Improvisations 29* and *30*. Later Müller recalled: "I did not know what it was, but I knew it was something." (*Ich wusste nicht, was es*

[4] Draft of a letter in English dated March 8, 1916, from Münter to Eddy, Gabriele Münter-und Johannes Eichner-Stiftung, Munich.

[5] Letter in English dated March 28, 1916, from Eddy to Kandinsky, Gabriele Münter- und Johannes Eichner-Stiftung, Munich.

*war, aber ich wusste, es war etwas.*)[6] In addition, the two collectors shared a liking for Chabaud's art.

Although installation photographs are lacking, we have some idea of how Eddy's collection was presented in his Chicago home. In March 1914 the society columnist of the *Chicago Daily Tribune* wrote that he does not "banish these strange, bewildering, amazing, and weirdly fascinating creations to a picture gallery. He and Mrs. Eddy live with them about in their daily life. Strange canvases hang in the reception room, study, dining room, and library; they throng the staircase walls almost impeding ascent and descent. There, for instance, as you go up, your elbow brushes the 'King and Queen Surrounded by Nudes,' the 'Game of Chess,' the 'Dance by the Spring,' and other old friends of last year's cubist show. Most post-impressionists are clustered in the second floor bedrooms, while the perfect expression of this school is reached by the curious and interesting collection of Kandinsky works which hang in the rather dim and dusky picture gallery on the third floor."[7] A photograph published in the newspaper that year (Figure 14.3) shows the collector standing on the stairs with Duchamp's *The King and Queen Surrounded by Swift Nudes* visible behind him.[8]

A few months later the artist Dawson recorded in his diary for May 25:

> Have been to Eddy's and have seen his big collection of paintings which he has hung in nearly every room in the house. It is somewhat indiscriminate. The newspapers have made a big notice of his having bought the 'Dance at the Spring' by Picabia and two or three Sousa-Cardoza [*sic*]. Cezanne [*sic*] is strangely missing and Picasso is represented only by a small, early, pointillist picture of an old Spanish woman. What a fine collection he could have with his money. One would think he would have something of Cezanne [*sic*], or Van Gogh, or De Gas [*sic*], or Gaugin [*sic*]. There is a little feeling as you look at the paintings with Eddy, of the possibility of the collection being to him a practical joke. His remark, with a

[6] Monique Barbier-Müller, "Der Sammler und die Seinen," in *Kunst über die Grenzen: Die Klassische Moderne von Cézanne bis Tinguely und die Weltkunst—aus der Schweiz gesehen*, eds. Christoph Vitali and Hubertus Gassner, exh. cat. (Munich: Haus der Kunst, 1999), 25–26.

[7] Mme X, "Comment by Mme. X," *Chicago Daily Tribune*, March 8, 1914, D2. She describes the Brancusi head as lying on the grand piano.

[8] "Arthur J. Eddy, Mayor's Appointee to Art Commission, and One of His Cubists," *Chicago Daily Tribune*, November 19, 1914, 5.

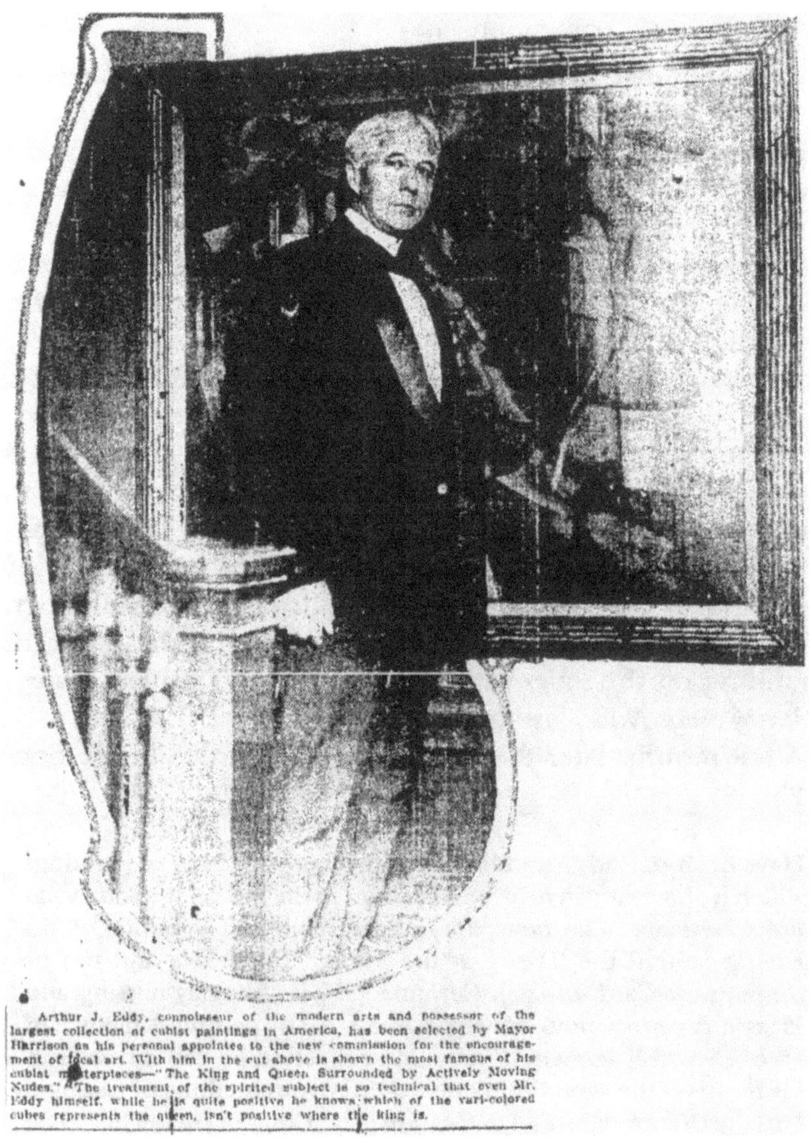

Arthur J. Eddy, connoisseur of the modern arts and possessor of the largest collection of cubist paintings in America, has been selected by Mayor Harrison as his personal appointee to the new commission for the encouragement of ideal art. With him in the cut above is shown the most famous of his cubist masterpieces—"The King and Queen Surrounded by Actively Moving Nudes." The treatment of the spirited subject is so technical that even Mr. Eddy himself, while he is quite positive he knows which of the vari-colored cubes represents the queen, isn't positive where the king is.

Figure 14.3 Photograph of Arthur J. Eddy and One of His Cubists.

*Chicago Daily Tribune*, November 19, 1914, 5. Image courtesy of the Chicago Public Library.

leer, that my two paintings would be excellent for Christmas presents, mentioning two of his friends he said "That will shock him."[9]

---

[9] Randy J. Ploog, Myra Bairstow, and Ani Boyajian, eds., *Manierre Dawson (1887–1969): A Catalogue Raisonné* (New York: The Three Graces, in association with Hollis Taggart Galleries, 2011), 146, 217–18, 304, 328. Dawson received payment for the two pictures in October 1914.

The paintings of Cézanne and the Post-Impressionists were no longer really new and were sought after by collectors—even the Metropolitan Museum purchased a Cézanne from the Armory Show. Their shock value was not as great as that of a Duchamp or a Kandinsky. Eddy was eager to discover what was new, unknown; and, yes, he delighted in shocking people. His goal was not to assemble a traditional collection, even a collection of modern art. In fact, he bought two radical works by Dawson, that he had asked the artist to bring when he came for dinner and saw the collection.

# XV

# Manierre Dawson, Charlotte Pollak, and the Americans

In the spring of 1914 at the Milwaukee Art Society, Eddy had seen Dawson's *Loop—Chicago* of 1910 and his five-sided canvas *Rotor* of 1913 in the *Exhibition of Paintings and Sculpture in "the Modern Spirit"* to which he lent several pictures from his own collection. Both of Dawson's works are lost, and no images are known. Eddy lent his Picabia *Dances at the Spring* (see Figure 10.7) as well as a group of drawings by Charlotte Pollak. Moreover, Eddy wrote a short text on her art: "The drawings by Miss Pollak are absolutely unique in this respect, they are the products of unfettered imagination ... all of Miss Pollak's drawings and paintings are as modern in spirit as anything exhibited in the International Exhibition last year, and yet up to the time of that exhibition she had never seen a modern picture, and had no idea that there was any one else in the world painting as she was painting." He explains that Pollak has lived most of her life in Alabama but that a trip to Canada, where she first saw Indians, inspired her to create works from her imagination. He attributes "the secret of the purity of her imaginative creations" to the fact that she is totally deaf. Eddy states that: "A more beautiful drawing than the 'Indians with Canoe' is not conceivable. The 'Indian Fugitive Lying in the Snow' is equally beautiful." He praises the beautiful color, charming design, and spontaneity of the work of this young woman in her twenties, who "is actually achieving what many of the extreme modern artists are attempting to do."[1]

Charlotte L. Pollak remains a virtually unknown artist. She was born in 1879 in Cullman, Alabama; attended the Clarke Institution for Deaf Mutes in Northampton, Massachusetts, in the 1890s along with her brother; took courses at the Art Students League in New York in 1911 with Kenneth Hayes Miller; exhibited with the Society of Independent Artists in New York in 1918–19; moved to the San Francisco area a few years later; and died at the Napa State Hospital in 1937, a psychiatric facility in California.[2]

Dawson's journal entry for the Milwaukee show on April 17, 1914, mentions Eddy again in a negative light and emphasizes his capriciousness: "The hallway took nice care of Charlotte Pollak's ten drawings. Eddy seems to set high store on these drawings as

---

[1] *Exhibition of Paintings and Sculpture in "the Modern Spirit,"* exh. cat. (Milwaukee Art Society, 1914), 9–10.

[2] I am grateful to Carol P. McCoy for providing information in 2010 and January 2011.

though he couldn't ever bear to part with them, yet he offered to sell me some."[3] We do not know when and how Eddy met Pollak, but it must have been in New York. We could dismiss her entirely except for the fact that Eddy owned more works by this unknown woman than by any other artist. Pictures are recorded in the inventory after the death of his widow, Lucy O. Eddy, in 1931 as hanging in the large ballroom on the third floor with Kandinskys and, in the 1937 auction, there are forty lots by Pollak. The present whereabouts of all of them are unknown. Two works appeared at auction in 2003 and on the basis of the reproductions of *Burlesque* (or *An Idea for a Vaudeville Act*) and *Indian Fugitive Lying in the Snow,*[4] Pollak's art neither looks very modern nor very imaginative.

Arthur Eddy began to acquire American art in 1893 and continued to purchase the work of living Americans at the Armory Show and afterward either directly from the artists or from galleries. After buying Kroll's *Terminal Yards* (see Figure 10.10) out of the Armory Show, he visited the artist's studio and chose eleven more pictures. Kroll remembered that "Arthur Jerome Eddy was a very interesting fellow. ... He thought I was the American white hope. That week I made ten thousand dollars, which was an enormous sum!"[5] In *Cubists and Post-Impressionism,* Eddy discussed two works by Kroll in the chapter on "Virile-Impressionism" (neither of which he owned) and considered him to be an Impressionist who "painted what he felt, *controlled* by what he saw."[6]

For years the best place to see modern art in New York was The Little Galleries of the Photo-Secession (known as *291*) that Alfred Stieglitz founded in 1905. Eddy invited Stieglitz to prepare the list of Exhibitions at 291 Fifth Avenue, which was published as Appendix I in *Cubists and Post-Impressionism.* The gallery showed Rodin drawings, Dove pastels, Brancusi sculptures, Picabia paintings, Marin watercolors, and Marsden Hartley's work. Around 1913 Eddy corresponded with Stieglitz, who was eager for him to purchase

[3] Manierre Dawson Journal, March 27, 1913, Manierre Dawson Papers, Archives of American Art. Transcribed in Randy J. Ploog, Myra Bairstow, and Ani Boyajian, eds., *Manierre Dawson (1887–1969): A Catalogue Raisonné* (New York: The Three Graces, in association with Hollis Taggart Galleries, 2011), 326.

[4] Treadway/Toomey, Chicago, 20th Century Art and Design Auction, September 7, 2003, lots 695, 699.

[5] Leon Kroll, *A Spoken Memoir,* eds. Nancy Hale and Fredson Bowers (Charlottesville: University of Virginia Press, 1983), 32.

[6] Arthur Jerome Eddy, *Cubists and Post-Impressionism* (Chicago: A. C. McClurg & Co., 1914), 210.

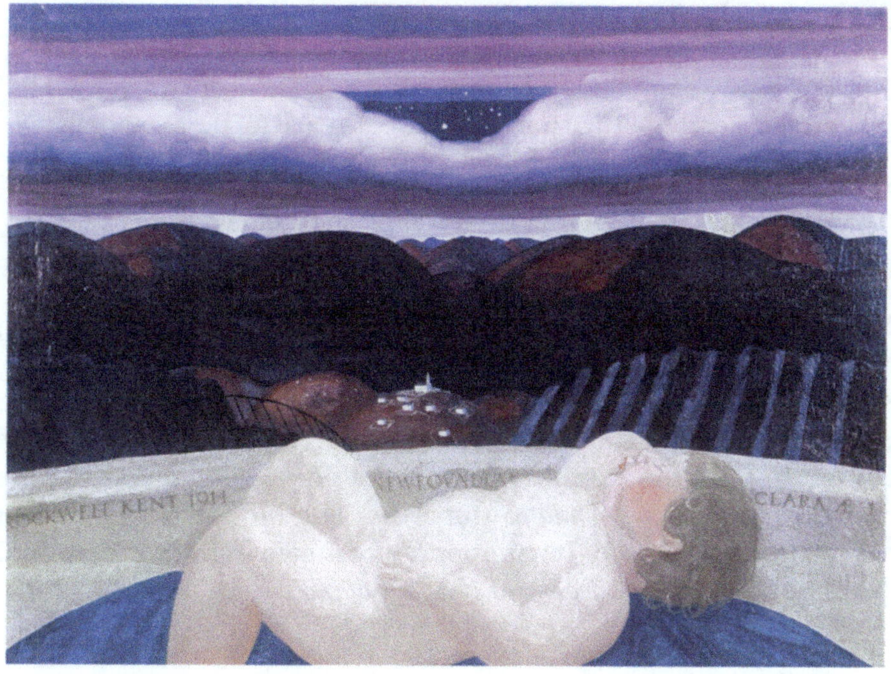

Figure 15.1 Rockwell Kent, *Portrait of a Child*, 1914.

State Pushkin Museum, Moscow. Photo courtesy of Scott R. Ferris. Copyright Scott R. Ferris, Susan Muniak, and Chameleon Books.

works by Hartley.[7] However, he never did; nor did he buy works by John Marin or Georgia O'Keeffe.

Even before the outbreak of the Great War in August 1914, dealers were promoting American art. In December 1913 Charles Daniel opened the Daniel Gallery at 2 West 47th Street, and the following year Stephan Bourgeois established the Bourgeois Gallery. Although both gallerists were of German descent, they featured American art, which many thought had not received sufficient recognition at the Armory Show. Daniel showed Kroll, Hartley, Marin, Kenneth Hayes Miller, Niles Spencer, Max Weber, and Rockwell Kent. He gave Charles Demuth, Preston Dickinson, and Man Ray their first one-man shows. In January 1915 Eddy purchased two paintings by Kent from Daniel: *Portrait of a Child* (Figure 15.1) and a Monhegan landscape. Daniel wrote the artist:

[7] Beinecke Rare Book and Manuscript Library, Yale University, New Haven, CT, Alfred Stieglitz/Georgia O'Keeffe Archive, YCAL MSS 85, Box 16, Folder 367.

> I have made some sales, among them Portrait of a Child and a Monhegan picture. The buyer is Mr. Eddy the Chicago collector, who buys prodigeously [*sic*] when he is interested and the prices are low. For the portrait framed I got $200.— and for the Monhegan 24 × 30 unframed 100.—I believe I might sell him others of your paintings. Please send a few more as soon as you can. Mr. Eddy makes frequent trips to New York, and I should like to have them here when he comes again.[8]

The child portrayed is the artist's daughter Clara, who was born in June 1914. The painting was shown in *A Representative Exhibition of American Art Today* at the Daniel Gallery, where Miller talked with Eddy. According to Miller, Eddy considered Kent's painting the best of those in the exhibition.[9] At some point Eddy seems to have returned *Portrait of a Child* to the artist. The Monhegan landscape has not been identified: It was apparently shown in Eddy's memorial exhibition in 1922 as *Dawn in Newfoundland.*

---

[8] Letter dated January 25, 1915, from Daniel to Kent, Rockwell Kent Papers, Archives of American Art, Smithsonian Institution, Washington DC, Reel 5173.

[9] Jake Milgram Wien, *Vital Passage: The Newfoundland Epic of Rockwell Kent*, exh. cat. (St. John's, Nova Scotia: The Rooms, 2014),13, 28.

# XVI

## Albert Bloch Exhibition, 1915

In January 1915 the American artist Albert Bloch had fourteen pictures shipped from Munich to Eddy in Chicago.[1] Of these, six were purchased by Eddy: *Prize Fight* (*Boxkampf*), *Harlequin* (*Harlekinade; Pantomime*), *Spring* (*Frühling*), *Song* (*Lied; Rocks*), *The Heights* (*Die Höhen*), and *Harlequin with Three Pierrots* (*Harklekin mit drei Pierrots*; Figure 16.1). Following Kandinsky's recommendation, the collector had already purchased several paintings, and now he was eager not only to acquire more, but also to arrange for an exhibition at the Art Institute. The show took place in July and August, then traveled to the City Art Museum of St. Louis in September. Eddy wrote the catalogue essay in which he characterizes Bloch's work as neither Cubist nor Futurist, but as "compositional painting." He situates Bloch as "one of a small group called the Blue Knights, headed by the Russian Kandinsky. ... The fundamental aim of the Blue Knights as a group is liberty of the individual to express himself in his own way, unhampered by juries, or other official or artificial restrictions."[2] He is careful to differentiate the work of Bloch, Kandinsky, and Marc and to emphasize the individuality of each artist. Eddy discusses eight of the paintings exhibited, describing *Night I* (Figure 16.2) as "almost a pure creation of the imagination as well as a beautiful composition of line and color" and *Summer Night* (see Figure 12.4) as "a purely poetic composition" that he envisions as a curtain in a theater. He observes that *Harlequin with Three Pierrots* (see Figure 16.1) is "one of his latest. It is looser in construction and freer in technic and probably marks a new development. It is essentially decorative, with a fine sweep of action."[3]

From Eddy's letters and essays about modern art, we deduce that he responds to brilliant color and the mysterious or poetic qualities of paintings that emerge only when looked at intently. In his essay on Bloch, Eddy articulates his view that the pictures "challenge our attention to themselves, and it is the verdict of everyone who happens to own some of the new paintings that they are most companionable, because they always reveal a little more and more, but never quite all of themselves. The best of them inwardly

[1] Copies of Bloch's Bilderlisten were consulted at the Max Kade Center at the University of Kansas in Lawrence in October 2013. I am most grateful to Frank Baron for generously assisting with my research.

[2] Arthur J. Eddy, *Catalogue of an Exhibition of Modern Paintings by Albert Bloch of Munich*, exh. cat. (Chicago: Art Institute of Chicago, 1915), 5–6.

[3] Eddy, *Catalogue*, 8–9.

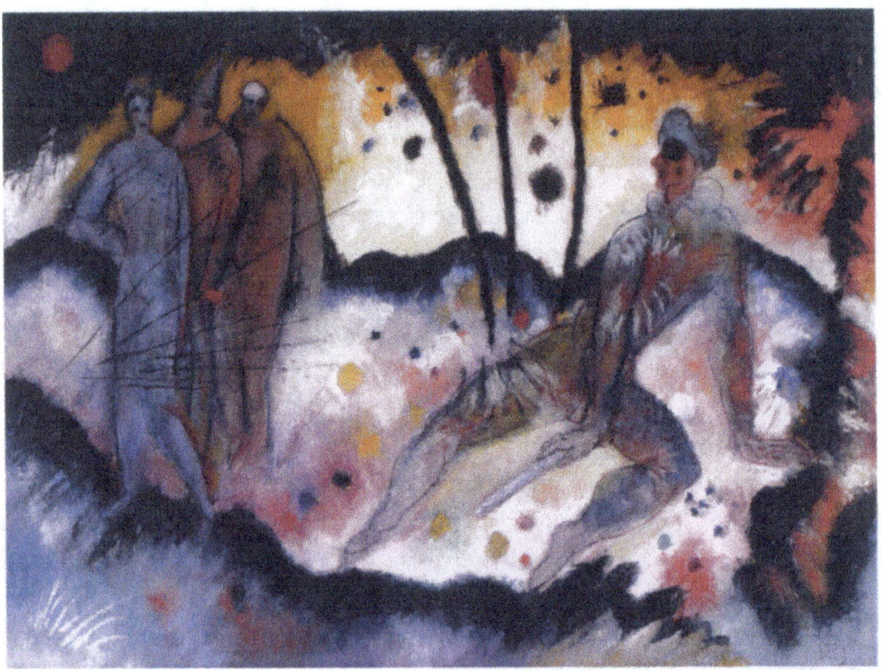

Figure 16.1 Albert Bloch, *Harlequin with Three Pierrots,* 1914.

The Art Institute of Chicago: Arthur Jerome Eddy Memorial Collection (1931.515)/Art Resource NY. © the Albert Bloch Foundation.

challenge our very best thought, while outwardly gratifying the eye with a brilliant harmony of line and color."

Years later the collector's son related that his parents' favorite painting was Bloch's *Night I* (see Figure 16.2).[4] The bursts of color set against the night sky give a dramatic feeling and enhance the expressiveness that Eddy appreciated. He owned at least twenty paintings by Bloch, ranging from a rather realistic *Boy with Orange* (*Knabe mit Apfelsine*) of 1911 to the gloomy but mystical *Figures on Dark Ground* (*Gestalten auf dunklem Grund*) of 1916 (Figure 16.3), both of which were included in the 1937 auction.

Eddy was the principal lender for the 1915 exhibition, but Mary Aldis (playwright, artist, and wife of his friend Arthur Aldis) lent a *Harlequin,* probably acquired because of their friend's enthusiasm.

[4] Letters dated April 12 and May 10, 1935, from Jerome O. Eddy to Earl Stendahl, Stendahl Art Galleries Records, Archives of American Art, Smithsonian Institution, Washington, DC, Reel 2717.

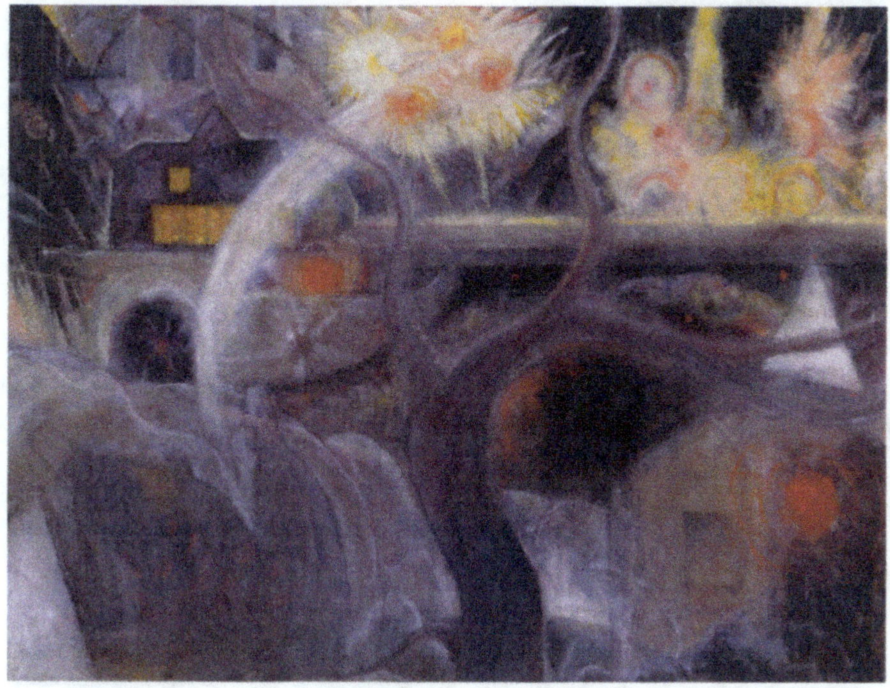

Figure 16.2 Albert Bloch, *Night I* (*Nacht 1*), 1913.

Fine Art Museums of San Francisco: M. H. de Young Museum, Museum purchase, American Art Trust Fund (2001.124). © the Albert Bloch Foundation.

Identification of Bloch's paintings is sometimes facilitated by the artist's Record Books, in which he catalogued in German most (but not all) of his paintings and illustrated them with black-and-white photographs.[5] Again in 1916, two more shipments of Bloch's paintings to Eddy were organized by the Galerie Der Sturm in Berlin via Carl Gummeson's gallery in Stockholm. Eddy bought more pictures: *Burial* (*Begräbnis*), *Garden in May* (*Der Garten im Mai*), *May: The Green Hillside* (*Mai—der grüne Hügel*), and *Figures on Dark Ground* (see Figure 16.3). In addition, William K. Bixby from St. Louis, the architect Franz Herding in St. Louis, and W. H. Mann of Cleveland purchased paintings; however, many works seem to have been returned. Eddy never met Bloch and, although they must have communicated, no correspondence survives.

[5] See Frank Baron and Jon Blumb, *Albert Bloch and the Blue Rider: The Munich Years* (Lawrence: Jayhawk Ink at the University of Kansas, 2014).

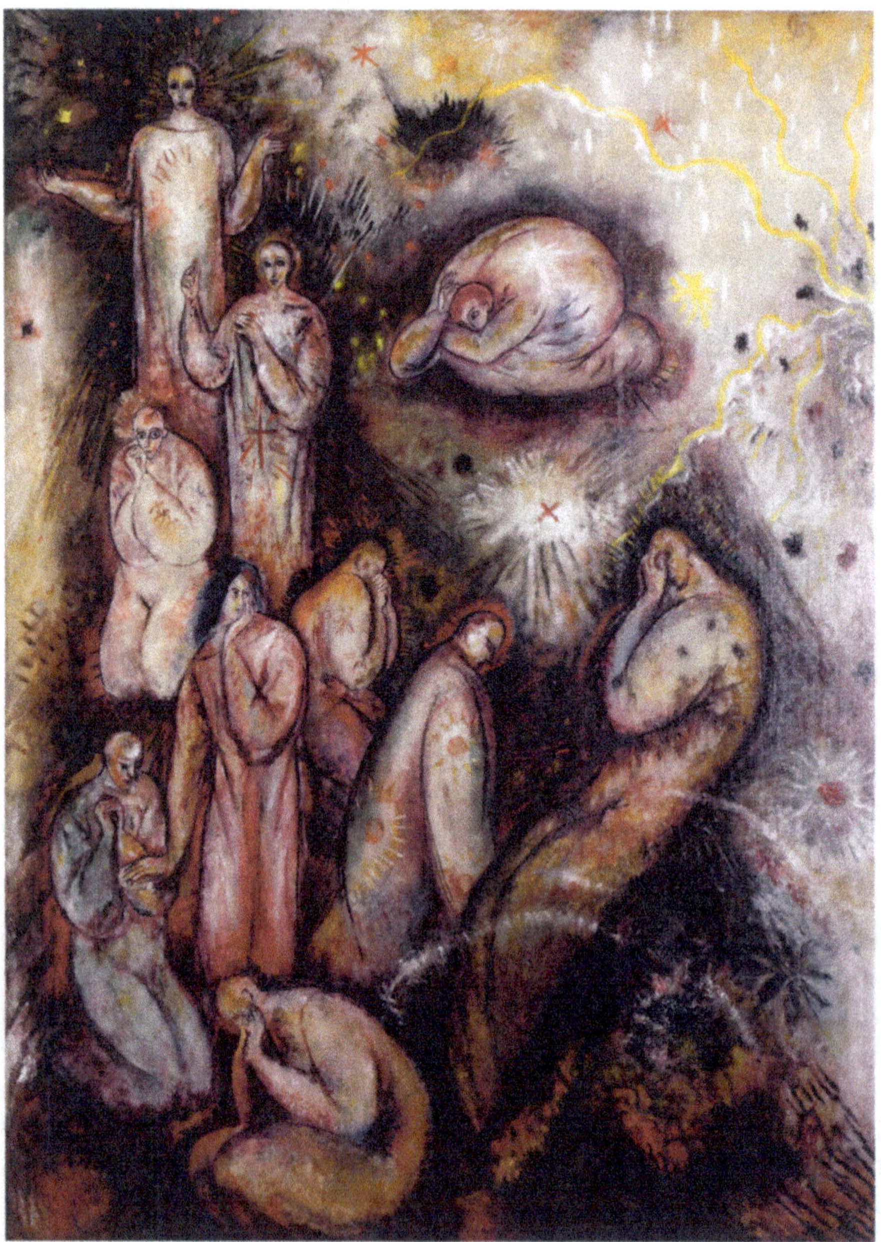

Figure 16.3 Albert Bloch, *Figures on Dark Ground,* 1916.

Courtesy Albrecht-Kemper Museum of Art, Gift of James and Virginia Moffett. © the Albert Bloch Foundation.

Even though Bloch was an American, he lived in Europe without encountering problems throughout the war years. As long as the United States remained neutral, art could travel to American galleries and collectors: for example, John Quinn purchased more pictures by Chabaud from the Carroll Galleries in New York in 1915.[6] It appears likely that Eddy also added works to his collection at that time. Certainly, after his death, there were more Chabauds and Van Reeses in his collection than what he had purchased in France before the war. Eddy's last trip to Europe was during the summer of 1913, after which he never returned.

[6] Véronique Serrano, "Biographie," in *Auguste Chabaud: la ville de jour comme de nuit,* exh. cat. (Marseille: Musée Cantini, 2003), 257.

# XVII

## More Americans: Man Ray, Charles Demuth, and Rockwell Kent

Not surprising, Eddy turned his attention to American artists. In November 1915, after the close of the Man Ray exhibition at the Daniel Gallery, he offered to buy six paintings from the artist for $2,000. Four from 1914 can be identified with certainty: *The Reaper* (Figure 17.1), *The Lovers, Four Figures in a Landscape,* and *Five Figures* (Figure 17.2). Born Emmanuel Radnitzky in Philadelphia in 1890, the artist was influenced by what he saw at the Armory Show and at Stieglitz's gallery. In three of the canvases, planimetric figures are presented within a two-dimensional space against an abstract background, whereas in *The Reaper* the landscape is more spacious and resembles the countryside where the artist lived in Ridgefield, New Jersey. In a questionnaire for the Whitney Museum of American Art, Man Ray wrote that *Five Figures* "was one of a series of compositions inspired by forms in "'primitive sculpture.'"[1] He would have seen African art not only reproduced in periodicals, but also at Stieglitz's gallery.

In December 1915 Charles Daniel hosted an exhibition of work by Marguerite and William Zorach. According to the latter, Eddy was so interested in their work that he arranged for a show at the O'Brien Gallery in Chicago and then went to visit the Zorachs in New York:

> He was kindled with enthusiasms and selected fifteen pictures from both of us and asked how much I wanted for them. For a minute I felt like a millionaire. Fifteen pictures. I figured I should get one hundred dollars a picture, so I said fifteen hundred dollars. He said, "I'll give you two hundred dollars for the lot." It was an awful shock to me. I said, "Mr. Eddy, I am not starving—There is a loaf of bread in the kitchen. Any one picture is worth more than you are offering me."

Later he told me that he bought a batch of paintings from a deaf mute girl studying art at the Art Students League for the two hundred dollars.[2] Thus, we learn more about the collector's connection to Pollak.

Eddy was in contact with Stieglitz in March 1916, when the gallerist sent an updated list of exhibitions at *291* for a new edition of

---

[1] The questionnaire dated March 23, 1957, is preserved in the Artists' Files at the Whitney Museum of American Art. See also Francis M. Naumann, *Conversion to Modernism: The Early Work of Man Ray*, exh. cat. (Montclair, NJ: Montclair Art Museum, 2003), 96.

[2] William Zorach, *Art Is My Life* (Cleveland, OH: World Publishing, 1967), 41–42.

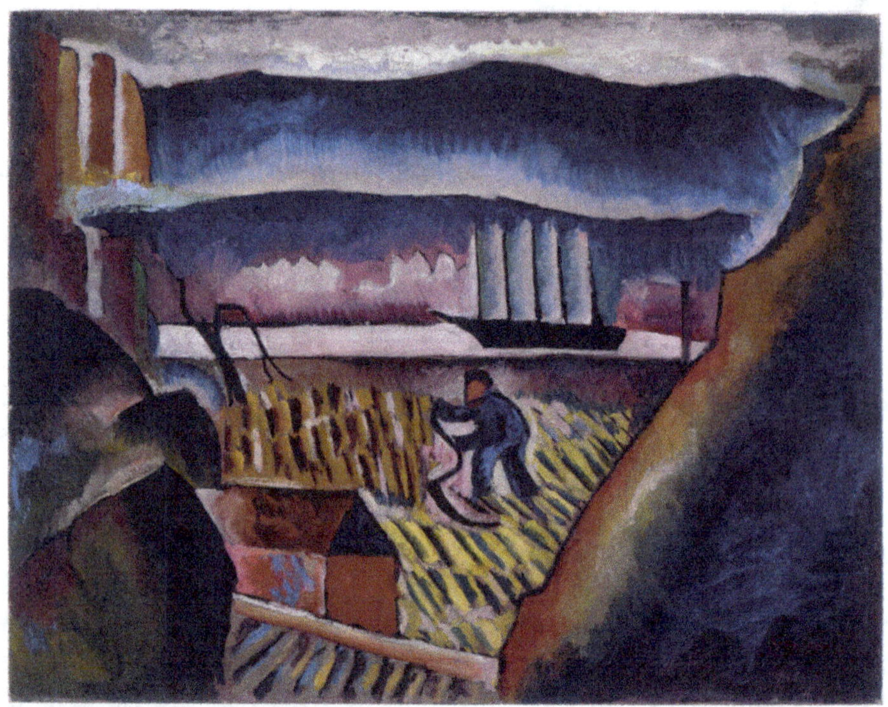

Figure 17.1 Man Ray, *The Reaper*, 1914.

Private collection, © 2019 Christie's Images Limited. Courtesy of Christie's, New York. © Man Ray 2015 Trust/ADAGP, Paris, 2022.

*Cubists and Post-Impressionism* and again urged Eddy to buy Hartley's paintings. The collector replied that he would "drop in and see the Hartleys; I always look forward to a *quiet hour* at '291.'"[3] Eddy did not purchase any work by Hartley or the Zorachs; in fact, he appears not to have bought anything from Stieglitz (nor did Quinn) although they often visited the gallery. After Stieglitz closed his gallery at 291 Fifth Avenue in June 1917, some artists (for example, John Marin, Stanton MacDonald-Wright, and Abraham Walkowitz) moved to the Daniel Gallery.

Daniel showed Kenneth Hayes Miller, Preston Dickinson, Charles Demuth, all of whom Eddy collected. Miller remembered seeing him at the gallery in January 1915 and probably Eddy acquired an unidentified painting by Miller referred to as "Disrobing" or

[3] Letter dated March 30, 1916, from Eddy to Stieglitz, Beinecke Rare Book and Manuscript Library, Yale University, New Haven, CT, Alfred Stieglitz/Georgia O'Keeffe Archive, Box 16, Folder 367.

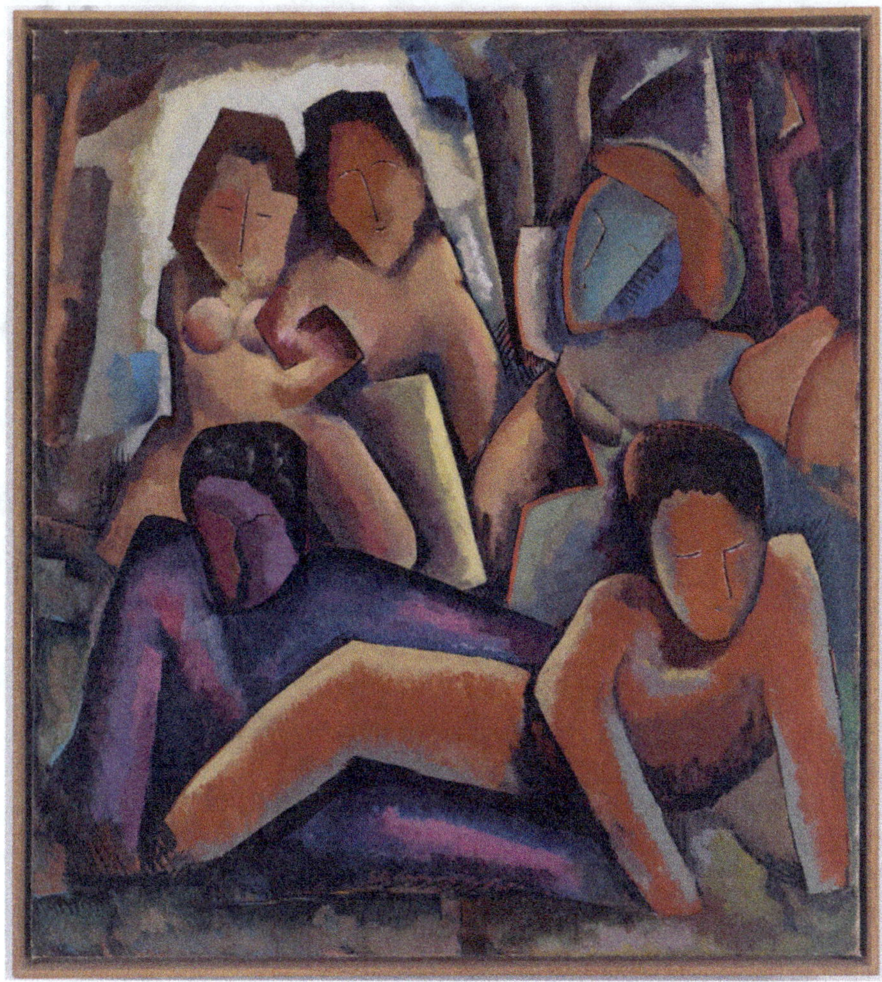

Figure 17.2 Man Ray, *Five Figures*, 1914.

Whitney Museum of American Art, New York: Gift of Katharine Kuh. © Man Ray 2015 Trust/ADAGP, Paris 2022. Digital image © Whitney Museum of American Art/Licensed by Scala/Art Resource, NY.

"Unveiling" between that time and 1918. Likewise, he owned a picture by Dickinson that was titled *Hillside* in the 1922 memorial exhibition. Eddy supposedly had two paintings and fifteen watercolors by Demuth.[4] In the 1931 inventory made after Lucy Eddy's

[4] Paul Kruty, "Arthur Jerome Eddy and His Collection: Prelude and Postscript to the Armory Show," *Arts Magazine* 61 (February 1987): 45; Kruty does not provide sources or titles. Neither oil has been located and to date only two watercolors can be identified.

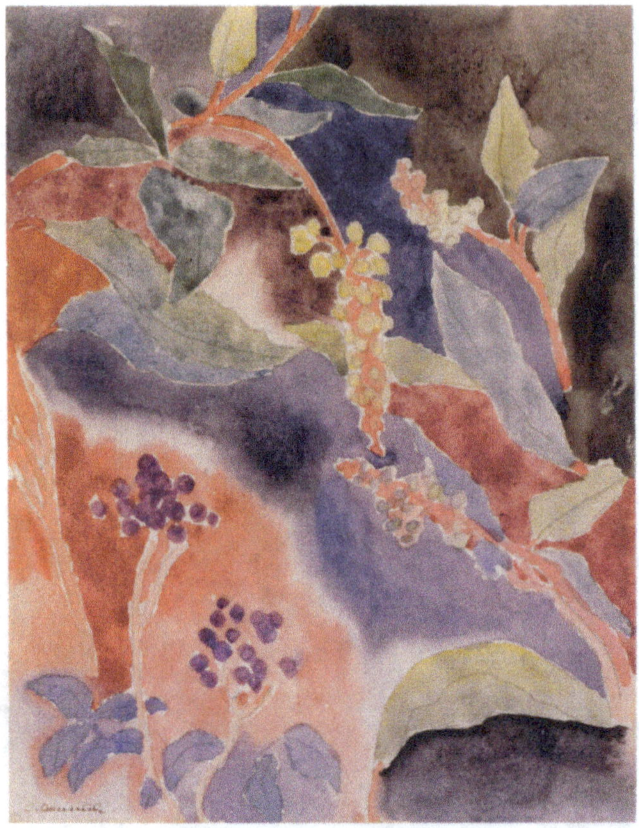

Figure 17.3 Charles Demuth, *Leaves and Berries*, c. 1915.

Detroit Institute of Arts: Gift of John S. Newberry, Jr./Bridgeman Images.

death, there are oils depicting "Nasturtiums" and "Forget-me-nots," which were probably Demuths, as well as twelve of his watercolors. Two of the artist's watercolors now in the Detroit Institute of Arts can be identified as having belonged to Eddy: *Leaves and Berries* (Figure 17.3) and *Flower Forms*.[5] Daniel had begun to show Demuth watercolors in 1914: he sold ten to Albert Barnes in 1917 and one to Louise and Walter Arensberg at about the same time.[6] The fact that neither Eddy's nor Daniel's papers exist makes it difficult, if not

[5] Emily Farnham, "Charles Demuth: His Life, Psychology and Works" (PhD diss., Ohio State University, 1959), vol. II, 458, 464.

[6] Richard Wattenmaker, *American Paintings and Works on Paper in the Barnes Foundation* (New Haven, CT: Yale University Press, 2010), 259, 266. See also Julie Mellby, *A Record of Charles Daniel and the Daniel Gallery* (Ann Arbor: University of Michigan Press, 1994), Appendix A.

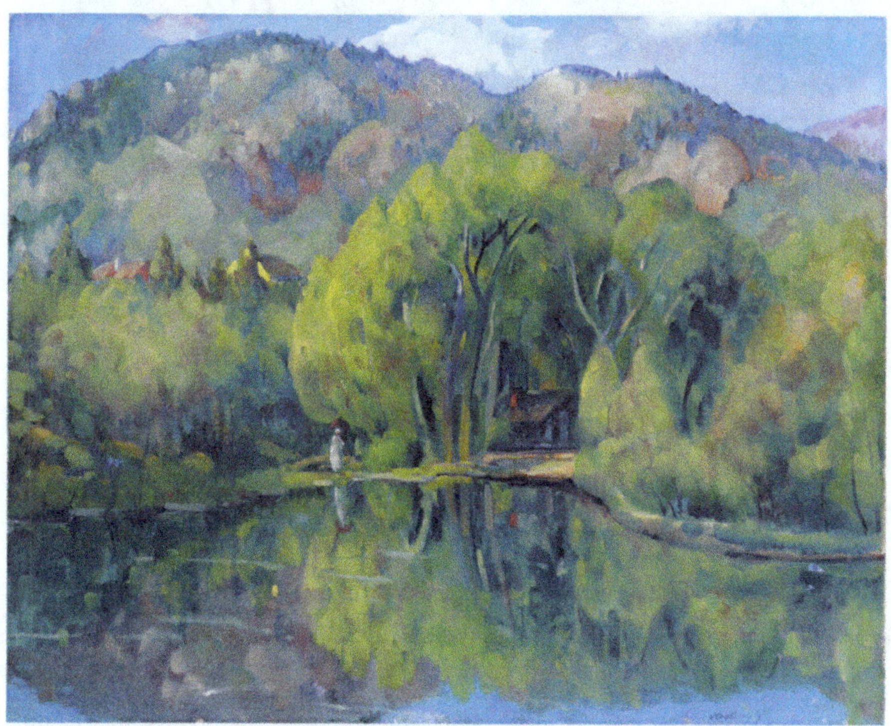

Figure 17.4 Leon Kroll, *The Lake in the Mountains*, 1917.

Private collection, Courtesy of Christie's, New York. © 2001 Christie's Images Limited.

impossible, to prove when and where many works were purchased.

Among the many American artists—in addition to those already mentioned—whose work Eddy favored and of which he had several examples, were Gifford Beal and Charles Fromuth. In addition, George Aid, Clifford Bend, Joseph Boston, Maurice Neven, Grace Ravlin, and Charles Rosen were all represented in the 1937 auction. William Wendt probably painted *Rocks and Sea* about 1897–1900 in California, but he lived and exhibited in Chicago at the turn of the century. Beal, Boston, Rosen, and Ravlin exhibited in Chicago before World War I. Gordon Stevenson's Italianate bas relief of the *Madonna and Child* was shown in Eddy's memorial exhibition in 1922.

Years after Eddy had purchased works from Kroll in 1913 at the time of the Armory Show, he added a painting dated 1917, *The Lake in the Mountains* (Figure 17.4), to his collection. In this case, we know that the canvas was exhibited at M. Knoedler in New York

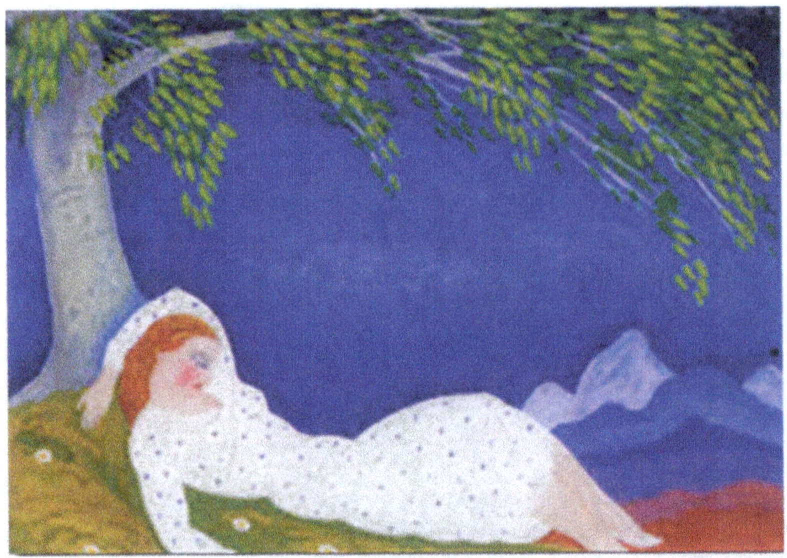

Figure 17.5 Rockwell Kent, *Girl Asleep Under a Tree,* 1917–18.

Collection of Jane and Douglas Smith. Photo by Mishalanie Photography. Photo courtesy of Scott R Ferris. Copyright Scott R Ferris, Susan Muniak, and Chameleon Books.

from late January to early February 1918. After the collector's death, the picture was given to the Flint Institute of Arts. It is softer and more idyllic than his earlier and more rugged *Terminal Yards* (see Figure 10.10), which Eddy acquired at the time of the Armory Show.

It was only in 1920 that Eddy obtained two glass paintings by Rockwell Kent, *Girl Asleep under a Tree* (Figure 17.5) and *Girl Tripping Downhill.* Both were included in the memorial show at the Art Institute in 1922. By then, Kent's canvas *Portrait of a Child* of 1914 (see Figure 15.1) had gone back to the artist, who later inscribed the painting to his friend, the composer Carl Ruggles, before giving it to the Soviet Union. The small paintings on the reverse of glass were done during the winter of 1917–18. The unusual technique used was popular in Bavarian folk art in the nineteenth and early twentieth centuries and was adopted by Jawlensky, Münter, Kandinsky, and Marc.

Eddy rarely sold works of art, but Duchamp's *The King and Queen Surrounded by Swift Nudes* (see Figure 10.6) was exhibited at the Bourgeois Gallery in New York in April 1916 and soon thereafter belonged to the Arensbergs; it was theirs certainly by 1919, when it appears in photographs that Charles Sheeler took of their New York apartment. Why Eddy decided to part with the painting is a mystery.[7] We know that other Cubist paintings by Picabia, Gleizes, Villon, and Duchamp hung in the main stairway leading from the first to the second floor of Eddy's house at the time of his death. At a later date, the collector's widow also sold Duchamp's *Portrait of Chess Players* (see Figure 10.4) to the Arenbergs.

[7] Carter H. Harrison, "Big Business Lawyer of Rebel Taste," *Chicago Evening Post*, December 29, 1931, 7. Harrison writes that Eddy "got a great kick from the sale of the 'King and Queen' at a big profit, not that he cared a whit for the money involved; he enjoyed the discomfiture of his critics who had prophesied for his ventures dire financial losses." However, Harrison's recollections tend not to be reliable.

# XVIII

## Final Years and Death

By 1918 Eddy was spending more time in New York. His law office was still located in the Temple in Chicago, but a New York address, 70 West 55th Street, also appears on his letterhead.[1] Newspapers cite his participation in chess games at the Manhattan Chess Club, bouts of sword dueling, and fencing competitions at the New York Athletic Club. In New York, Eddy belonged to the Metropolitan Club as well as the Athletic Club. In Chicago, he was active in the Cliff Dwellers Club and the Arts Club. He was in frequent contact with the poet Harriet Monroe. In 1916–17, Lucy Eddy was not well and more than once underwent treatment for "her nerves" in Baltimore.[2] Arthur Eddy went to visit her there on weekends while staying in New York. In fact, he had leased a room at the Hotel Devon, which was located at 70 West 55th Street.

In 1918 Eddy wrote to Stieglitz that he was "at last taking the time to finish my revision of the second edition of the Cubist book." Although he did not try to expand the bibliography, he asked Stieglitz to update the list of exhibitions at *291* and to write a final paragraph. By then, the gallery had closed. Eddy wrote that he had stopped in one day and was told that "you had given up the gallery. I was mighty sorry to hear it."[3]

The second and revised edition of *Cubists and Post-Impressionism* was published in November 1919 by A. C. McClurg & Co. Eddy wrote a new foreword, which he thought was "about as good a thing as there is in the book." In the same letter he also told Stieglitz: "There are a good many revisions of the book and some additions to the text, but on the main the book is very much as it was, and I regret to say that it is about as poorly bound as was the first edition."[4] He added one illustration (a sculpture by Henri Gaudier-Brzeska), updated a few footnotes as well as the index, and expanded the chapter on "Virile-Impressionism."

The 1919 edition relates how Kandinsky wrote enthusiastically about Bloch and how "with invaluable assistance of Messrs. Arthur

[1] Letter dated May 20, 1918, from Eddy in Chicago to Stieglitz in New York, Beinecke Rare Book and Manuscript Library, Yale University, New Haven, CT, Alfred Stieglitz/Georgia O'Keeffe Archive, Box 16, Folder 367. The same letterhead was used by Jerome O. Eddy in his letter dated July 28, 1920, preserved in the Archives of the Art Institute.

[2] Letter dated March 28, 1917, from Eddy to Monroe, is preserved with *Poetry: A Magazine of Verse* (Box 44, Folder 22), Special Collection, Research Center, University of Chicago Library.

[3] Letter dated May 20, 1918, from Eddy in Chicago to Stieglitz, Beinecke Rare Book and Manuscript Library, Yale University, New Haven, CT, Alfred Stieglitz/Georgia O'Keeffe Archive, Box 16, Folder 367.

[4] Letter dated April 26, 1920, from Eddy to Stieglitz, Beinecke Rare Book and Manuscript Library, Yale University, New Haven, CT, Alfred Stieglitz/Georgia O'Keeffe Archive, Box 16, Folder 367.

T. Aldis, Howard Shaw, and Frederic C. Bartlett, an exhibition of twenty-five of Bloch's paintings was arranged at the Chicago Art Institute for the summer of 1915."[5] Eddy discusses several works in the show (all of which he owned): *Factory Chimneys, Clowns II, Summer Night* (see Figure 12.4), *Lamentation (Klagelied)*, *Harlequin with Three Pierrots* (see Figure 16.1), *Night I* (see Figure 16.2), and *Figures on Dark Ground* (see Figure 16.3). He then reveals that:

> I have lived with Kandinsky's and Bloch's pictures several years and like them more and more. They practically line the side walls of a room at one end of which hangs a full length Manet and at the other end a full length Whistler—neither artists nor laymen have ever noted or seemed to feel any conflict. The brilliant canvasses [*sic*] make a fine setting for the two more sober [pictures], illustrating the fact that *good paintings* of all schools, and all times hang together.[6]

Eddy's foreword to the new edition of *Cubists and Post-Impressionism* focuses on the Great War. Rather than dwelling on the events that led to the war, he proposes that a "profounder [*sic*] and more philosophical searcher ... may reach the conclusion that the development of the western world had reached a condition where an explosion was inevitable."[7] He writes that "one of the bright sides of the war is the superb way our Government is bursting century-old shackles" and concludes that politically and aesthetically "we are in a period of post-traditionalism. ... It is good to be alive in a post-traditional epoch."[8]

The war made communication with Europe extremely difficult, which affected revisions to Eddy's book, shipment of artworks, and other travel was quite impossible. From the *Chicago Daily Tribune* in 1917 we learn that Eddy's power yacht *Minnemac II* was to be turned over to the government as a submarine chaser.[9] Also that year he published an article on bond levies as a war debt panacea, arguing for a revision of the existing tax system to spread the burden equally on all classes and remove the danger of repudiation or national

[5] Arthur Jerome Eddy, *Cubists and Post-Impressionism*, rev. ed. (Chicago: A. C. McClurg & Co., 1919), 201.

[6] Eddy, *Cubists*, rev. ed., 205.

[7] Eddy, *Cubists*, rev. ed., vii.

[8] Eddy, *Cubists*, rev. ed., ix.

[9] "Arthur Eddy's Yacht to Be Submarine Chaser," *Chicago Daily Tribune*, June 2, 1917, 2.

bankruptcy.[10] Moreover, law firms had to reorganize when partners entered or left the army. In February 1918 Eddy was named counsel to the newly formed law firm of Dickinson, Wetten & Keehn.[11] A year later Wetten & Matthews was established with offices in The Temple after Dickinson, Wetten & Keehn was dissolved. Emil C. Wetten had been Eddy's partner for at least fifteen years as the law firm evolved. The newspaper reported that Arthur J. Eddy would continue at the same address.[12]

Even after the war ended, Eddy did not travel to Europe. He was occupied with updating not only *Cubists and Post-Impressionism* but was also preparing a new edition of *The New Competition;* and was writing a new book, *Property*, which appeared posthumously in July 1921 (Figure 18.1). In many ways *Property* goes back to the ideas about human nature and communities that he had expressed in *The New Competition.* The introduction begins with a quotation from Pierre-Joseph Proudhon: "What is property? Property is theft." As he had with competition, Eddy posits that "the institution of property has been on the whole a vital factor in the progress of mankind."[13] He states that inequality is not confined to the distribution of wealth; it exists everywhere, and he makes a distinction between paper wealth and actual wealth (composed of land and luxuries). To Eddy, every evil known to society has its origin in and derives its strength from the individual.[14] His examples of those with enormous wealth are John D. Rockefeller, Andrew Carnegie, Russell Sage, Marshall Field, and Henry C. Frick. Emphasizing the role of philanthropy and how much money Mrs. Sage gave back to the public, Eddy views the luxuries of wealth from the standpoint of the community rather than the individual. In the preface to the book, Horace J. Bridges considers Eddy to have been a teacher and intellectual leader and praises his "certain alert openness of soul, a youthful responsiveness to the challenge of new ideas, new experiments, new valuations."[15]

While in New York on business in July 1920, Eddy was hospitalized with severe appendicitis. He died on July 21 at age sixty after surgery at Post Graduate Hospital in Manhattan. The funeral was

[10] Arthur J. Eddy, "Sees Bond Levies a War Debt Panacea," *Annalist* 10, no. 254 (November 26, 1917): 678–79.

[11] *Chicago Daily Tribune*, February 11, 1918, 10.

[12] *Chicago Daily Tribune*, March 27, 1919, 5.

[13] Arthur Jerome Eddy, *Property* (Chicago: A. C. McClurg & Co., 1921), 1–3.

[14] Eddy, *Property*, 53–55.

[15] Eddy, *Property*, i.

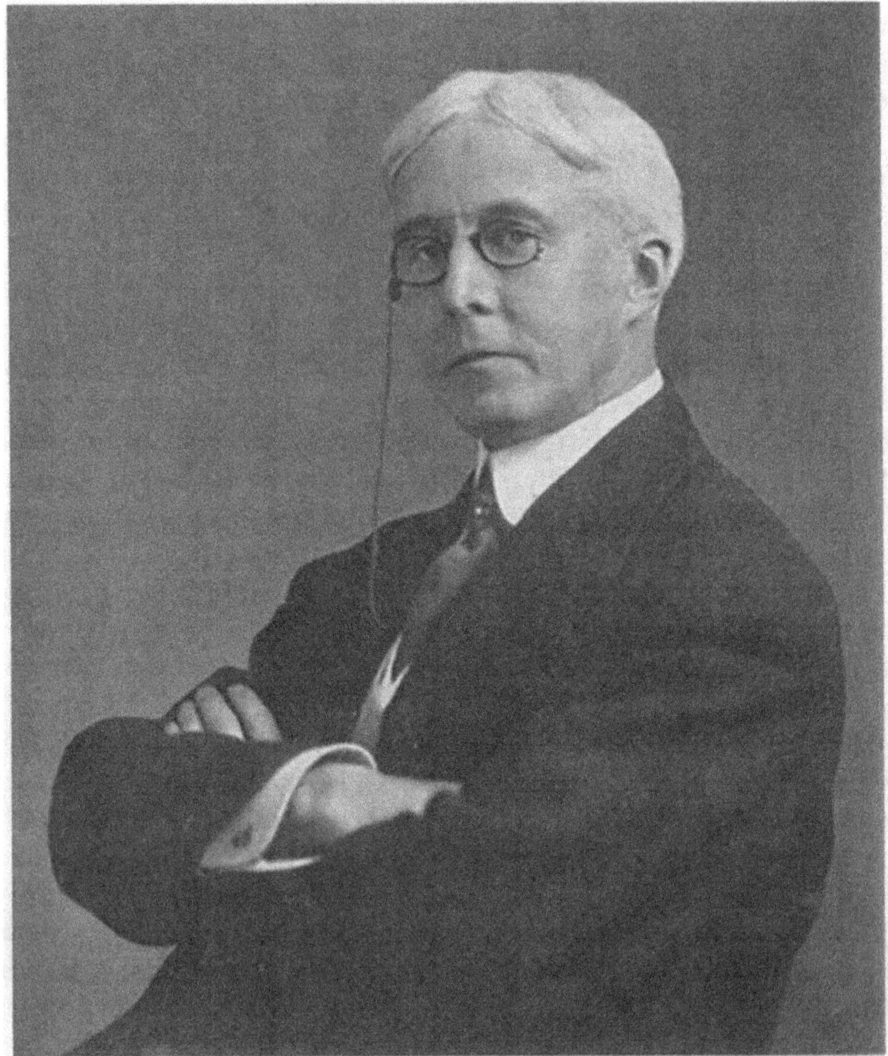

Figure 18.1 Photograph of Arthur Jerome Eddy published as the frontispiece in his book *Property*, 1921.

Photo courtesy New York Public Library Digital Collections.

held in Flint at the home of his mother, Mrs. Jerome A. Eddy, and he was buried in Glenwood Cemetery there. Eddy's obituary in the *Chicago Daily Tribune* referred to him as a "lawyer, organizer of large industries, pioneer automobilist, globe trotter, author, and Chicago's foremost art critic." It mentioned that his two residences were filled with art treasures, and that "his office on the eighth floor of the Woman's Temple is a miniature art gallery."[16] The *Pasadena Star-News* quoted his neighbor and close friend Judge G. A. Gibbs: "Mr. Eddy was a man of most unusual versatility, one who seemed able to make the greatest success of everything he undertook. He was also a man of greatest personal charm."[17] *The Iron Age* cited his many accomplishments and emphasized his ideas on open pricing:

> It is hard to overestimate the influence Mr. Eddy exerted in his direction of the discussions at the monthly meetings of the numerous organizations for which he acted as counsel. His attitude was such as to discourage pettiness and to encourage his associates to adopt a broad vision in the conduct of their affairs. His advice was always wholesome and his attitude toward any attempt at illegal practises was one of intolerance. ... The delight of association with Mr. Eddy arose from the fact that while he was intensely practical on the one hand, he was no less absorbed in the subject of art, in the fields of literature, and in the solution of public questions. It was impossible to converse with him for any length of time without being lifted out of the rut of commercial aloofness.[18]

[16] *Chicago Daily Tribune*, July 22, 1920, 7.
[17] *Pasadena Star-News*, July 22, 1920, 20.
[18] *The Iron Age*, 106 (July 29, 1920): 297.

# XIX

## Dispersal of the Collection

On November 1, 1920, the executors of the Estate of Arthur J. Eddy, namely, his son, Jerome O. Eddy, and The Northern Trust Company, submitted a bill of appraisement to the Probate Court of Cook County Illinois.[1] The inventory of the furnishings and equipment lists the contents of the house at 4152 Sheridan Road room by room, paying more attention to household items in the pantries than to works of art and books. Nevertheless, it provides some evidence for where objects were located.

The reception hall showed figure paintings by George Aid, Henry Lerolle, Henry Oliver Walker as well as garden views by Gaston Lhuer and Robert Vonnoh. Eddy's study contained sixteen oil paintings, ten works on paper, and approximately 1,220 books. Among the paintings were Van Rees's *Still Life* (illustrated in *Cubists and Post-Impressionism*), a *Still Life* by Herbin, a Chabaud portrait, two Man Rays, and a watercolor by Mary Aldis. In the living room, Harrison's *Moonlight Marine* and Ochtman's *Along the Mianus River* (see Figure 4.3) were hung with pictures of boats by Alfred Stevens and Charles Fromuth. The dining room presented landscapes by Monet (see Figure 4.7), Bloch, and John Constable; a small village scene by Jean-François Raffaelli; Derain's *Forest at Martigues* (see Figure 10.8); and a Cubist landscape probably by Herbin (see Figure 9.2). Although we know when Eddy purchased the Harrison, Monet, Herbins, and Derain, there is no indication of when or where he acquired the Constable or the Raffaelli.

In the inventory, the stairway to the second floor specifically refers to Marcel Duchamp and the other works can be identified with Cubist pictures by Gleizes, Picabia, Segonzac, and Villon. In Eddy's bedroom there was a landscape with cows in a stream by James McDougal Hart as well as a factory scene by Bloch and a picture with five figures (perhaps by Man Ray). By the time the appraisers reached the third floor, they rarely provided subjects of paintings and names of artists: there were works by Bloch, Chabaud, Kandinsky, and Münter. More attention was paid to the frames than to what was inside them. Large Kandinskys were appraised at $25, whereas the highest value listed ($500) was assigned to Lerolle's *On the Field.* There was a detailed list of liquor, wine, and champagne (for which no market value could be given according to law). The goods and chattels listed in the bill of appraisement totaled $22,814. The total value of his estate was appraised at less than $500,000.

[1] Cook County Probate Court file P66345, doc. 197, p. 187.

Eddy's will was dated May 20, 1913, and witnessed by his partners Charles H. Pegler and Jasper F. Rommel in the firm of Eddy, Wetten & Pegler. It did not mention individual works of art but bequeathed "the remaining one-fourth (1/4), and any bequest which may have lapsed for want of beneficiaries to the Trustees of the Art Institute of Chicago with which to encourage by prizes and purchases the production of painting and sculpture, especially decorative and architectural, in America by native Americans working and residing in this country. (This restriction is made because production by native workers is not encouraged as it should be, and, of all workers, they are usually in the greatest need.)" In 1913 the term *native Americans* would have meant people born in the United States. Further clarification of the bequest was provided by Emil C. Wetten and conveyed to the museum's president by the curator:

> The Art Institute will not receive any benefit from the bequest until after the decease of Mrs. Eddy and Jerome Eddy, who is about twenty-eight years of age, so that we cannot expect much in this way. However, it is the intention of the mother and son as soon as the Will is probated to try to carry out some of Mr. Eddy's ideas and assist the Art Institute in the purchase of works of art. They will then have a conference with us.[2]

Eddy had, in fact, prepared a new will that he planned to sign on July 24, the very day of his funeral. Evidently, his widow and son intended to follow the terms of his second unsigned will, which bequeathed more to the Art Institute.[3]

At the time of his death Arthur Eddy was a Governing Member of the museum: He had been one earlier and asked in February 1917 that he be reinstated. After his death it was Arthur Aldis—and his wife, Mary—who brought up the possibility that the collection might be offered to the Art Institute.[4] The Director, Robert Harshe, and the Trustees visited the collection in June 1922; then Mr. Harshe arranged for sixty-seven works to be brought to the museum on

[2] Letter dated July 30, 1920, from C. V. Burkholder, Curator of Exhibitions, to Charles L. Hutchinson, President of the Art Institute. Copy of the will and related correspondence preserved with Arthur Jerome Eddy Memorial Collection in the Archives of the Art Institute.

[3] "A. J. Eddy Heirs to Follow Will He Never Signed," *Chicago Daily Tribune*, August 3, 1920, 17.

[4] Letter dated June 26, 1922, from Arthur T. Aldis to Robert Harshe, Director's File, Archives of the Art Institute.

loan for a memorial exhibition that autumn.[5] The catalogue listed sixty-three paintings and four sculptures and included excerpts from Eddy's writings.

Nine years later the Art Institute presented an exhibition of The Arthur Jerome Eddy Memorial Collection with twenty paintings and three sculptures given to the museum by his widow and son. The catalogue essay by Daniel Catton Rich, a young member of the curatorial staff (later the museum's director), praised Mr. Eddy as "an enthusiast for all that was new and vital in life. As a collector, Eddy was absolutely courageous."[6] The text emphasized modern art—works that had been in the Armory Show (see Figures 10.1, 10.5, 10.8, 10.9, 10.11, 10.14, and 10.15) as well as paintings by Kandinsky (see Figures 11.3, 11.6, and 12.6) and Marc (see Figure 11.10). Lucy Orrell Eddy did not live to see the opening of the exhibition at the Art Institute: She died on August 27, 1931. Under the terms of her will, eight more traditional artworks were bequeathed to the Flint Institute of Arts. Later, her son, Jerome, made additional gifts to the museum in Flint.[7]

After the death of Mrs. Eddy, there was an appraisal[8] of the contents of the house on Sheridan Road in September 1931, which, studied together with the 1920 inventory taken after her husband's death, sheds further light on works of art as well as books. The same pictures were still in the reception hall with the addition of a Gifford Beal. The living room was unchanged, but the Derain no longer hung in the dining room. Although the 1920 inventory is minimal, changes seem to have been made to Mr. Eddy's study and former bedroom. Most striking is the omission of the Duchamp from the staircase, which had been moved to the second floor. In 1931 the appraisers attempted to read the signatures and dates on paintings, describe the objects, and take their measurements: Thus, many works by Kandinsky, Münter, Jawlensky, Bloch, Kroll, and even Pollak can be identified in the third-floor ballroom. The greater detail extended to the books where the works of Honoré de Balzac, Charles

[5] The Art Institute of Chicago, Exhibition of Paintings from the Collection of the Late Arthur Jerome Eddy, September 19–October 22, 1922.

[6] Daniel Catton Rich, The Art Institute of Chicago, *Exhibition of the Arthur Jerome Eddy Collection of Modern Paintings and Sculpture, December 22, 1931–January 17*, exh. cat. (Chicago: Art Institute of Chicago, 1932), 4.

[7] Among the works donated to the Flint Institute of Arts are Figures 2.1, 4.3, 4.4, 4.8, 6.1, 10.10, and 17.4.

[8] Cook County Probate Court file 168934, doc. 308, p. 618.

Dickens, Ralph Waldo Emerson, Gustave Flaubert, Rudyard Kipling, John Ruskin, William Shakespeare, and many others are catalogued.

Probably while preparing the 1931 exhibition, Mr. Rich wrote a short unpublished text[9] in which he described visiting the Eddys' house.

> Once inside the procedure was always the same. You were met by a butler bearing a reading-lamp and reflector with a reel of electric cord. In his hand was a typewritten catalogue of the pictures, set down in Eddy's most pointed style. Slowly you made the rounds of the dim first floor; the reading lamp flashed on one painting at a time. The beginning was mild. A Gifford Beal circus scene sticks in the memory, then in quick succession, a Derain of the Fauve period, and some of the more conventional works of Albert Bloch. ... The climax was made in the ballroom. In other parts of the house the pictures had been tolerated; here they had taken complete possession. From base-board to ceiling they were plastered on the walls, with not a square inch of background visible. When the lights were raised the room burst into a storm of color. A series of Kandinskys, from the early decorative style through the brilliant "spatula" period, reached their climax in a large square canvas, Improvisation No.30. A kaleidoscopic Franz Marc, a simpler early one.

Mr. Rich mentions pictures by Duchamp, Picabia, Gleizes, Münter, Jawlensky, Van Rees plus "paintings by Rockwell Kent, Arthur B. [*sic*] Dove, Preston Dickinson, and a group by Leon Kroll. Only twice did the waves of color part, subside. At one end hung a Manet 'Philosopher,' in the dark green and brown of his Spanish period; at the other, a Whistler portrait of Eddy himself, very grey, always wan in such a company." Nearby was Rodin's portrait bust of Eddy, which "for all its seeming vigor, was deficient in the sort of personal strength Eddy must have possessed."

No trace remains of a typed inventory, but from the appraisals and the checklist for the 1937 auction it is possible to reconstruct most of what was in the collection. During the thirties Jerome O. Eddy and his wife, Effie, were in contact with the Stendahl Gallery in Los Angeles and tried to sell works from his father's collection. Earl Stendahl took works by Chabaud, Beal, Pollak, Kroll, and other

[9] Daniel Catton Rich, "Arthur Jerome Eddy—Portrait of a Collector," unpublished manuscript consulted in Department of Medieval Modern European Painting and Sculpture, Art Institute of Chicago, on March 9, 2011.

artists. He sold Marc's *Red Deer I* (see Figure 11.9) and Kandinsky's *Murnau—Village Street* of 1908 to the movie director Josef von Sternberg, but his most significant clients were Louise and Walter Arensberg, who had moved to Hollywood in 1921. The Arensbergs had already acquired both of Eddy's Duchamps and they bought his Villon in 1932. From Stendahl they purchased the Picasso (see Figure 9.1) as well as two Kandinskys (see Figures 11.2 and 12.7) in 1934 and, over the next two years, the Picabia (see Figure 10.7) and Gleizes (see Figure 10.2).

From the correspondence with Earl Stendahl,[10] it is clear that Jerome and Effie, who lived in New Mexico and, before moving near Prescott, Arizona, in 1935, wanted to sell art that his father had collected that "is out of place here in the ranch house and will be more so in the smaller new home." As his wife told Stendahl: "I think we have already practically given the paintings away so I would not be interested in low prices. Both Jerry and I do not want to trade as we want money for the paintings—already having more than we need of paintings we did not choose."[11] They complained about the low prices works brought and about paying for warehouse space at Hebard in Chicago (where 160 works were stored in January 1934).[12]

Jerome arranged for an auction of "modernistic paintings and antique Oriental rugs" on January 20, 1937, at Williams, Barker & Severn on South Wabash Avenue in Chicago.[13] Numerous works by Kandinsky, Münter, Bloch, Chabaud, Pollak, and Van Rees appear on the minimal printed list. The art dealers Katharine Kuh and Leo Buntman bought works: She snatched up several paintings by Kandinsky, Jawlensky, and Man Ray (see Figures 11.5, 11.7, and 17.1). The British vice consul John Thwaites and his wife bought the Dove pastel and a large Kandinsky painting from 1914. Kuh, who was later a curator at the Art Institute, remembered that "the auctioneer had no idea what he was selling. The first thing he said was, 'What am I bid for this Tinpansky?' It was a handsome

---

[10] Stendahl Art Galleries Records, Archives of American Art, Smithsonian Institution, Washington DC, Reel 2717.

[11] Letter dated November 3, 1937, from Effie Eddy to Earl Stendahl, Archives of American Art, Smithsonian, Washington, DC.

[12] Letter dated January 3, 1934, from Jerome Eddy to Earl Stendahl, Archives of American Art, Smithsonian, Washington, DC.

[13] Williams, Barker & Severn Co., "Art Auction by order of Jerome O. Eddy, Skull Valley, Arizona, Son of the late Arthur J. Eddy," annotated copy in Department of the Registrar, Art Institute of Chicago.

Expressionist painting by Kandinsky, a 1909 landscape of a church in Murnau [see Figure 11.5]. The auctioneer suggested twenty dollars. I nodded, and he said, 'Sold!'" She recalled that "thanks to his breezy ignorance, I acquired ten pictures" paying five dollars for another Kandinsky and ten dollars for a Man Ray.[14] Many works were unsold and storage at Hebard on Sheridan Road was discontinued. Some of the Jawlenskys and Münters are unaccounted for as are pictures by Chabaud, Dickinson, Genin, Kent, and Van Rees. Moreover, whatever happened to the Klees, Dawsons, and Demuths, which did not come up for auction and of which there is no trace?

The scattering of Arthur Jerome Eddy's collection is regrettable, even tragic, as it obliterates much of his legacy. Over a period of twenty-five years he assembled an incredibly personal collection without the assistance of curators or art advisors. At certain times, he relied on artists: Whistler and Kandinsky. When he started in 1893, Eddy may have followed what other Chicagoans collected; yet in 1915 it was he who presented Cubist paintings to Bertha Honoré Palmer in his home.[15] At the beginning and again in his last years, Eddy bought primarily American art but within a larger European context. His American artists encompassed Henry Oliver Walker, Winslow Homer, William Wendt, Leon Kroll, Rockwell Kent, and Man Ray. After the Armory Show he did not buy more Cubist work; in fact, he did not own many Fauve or Cubist pictures. His taste for French art extended from Lerolle and Lhuer to Duchamp and Picabia. No one else in America admired and acquired Expressionist painting from Munich as he did. Throughout his life, Arthur Jerome Eddy chose what he liked, what spoke to him.

---

[14] Katharine Kuh and Avis Berman, *My Love Affair with Modern Art* (New York: Arcade Publishing, 2006), 12–13.

[15] *Chicago Daily Tribune*, December 25, 1915, 15.

# Index

Page numbers in *italics* refer to illustrations.

**L**

www.ingramcontent.com/pod-product-compliance
Lightning Source LLC
LaVergne TN
LVHW081600100826
845153LV00004B/426

* 9 7 8 1 6 0 6 1 8 1 1 2 6 *